Brighten Your Corner

My Life Making Music in Mason County, Kentucky

By Coralie Runyon Jones

*This book would not have been possible without the
encouragement of my children:
Randy, for his careful editing and
Connie, for her recollections and encouragement.
I would also like to thank Elizabeth, my daughter-in-law and
former student, for her skill in editing and preparing the manuscript
for publication. Also thanks to the Mason County Museum Center
for making available various newspaper files.*

Copyright © Coralie Runyon Jones, 2006.
All rights reserved.

Cover art:
Detail from an original painting by Catherine Smart Wells, 1932 Simon Kenton Suspension Bridge over the Ohio River from Maysville, Kentucky, to Aberdeen, Ohio. Used with permission of the artist.

ISBN 0-9786978-0-4

Printed in the United States of America.

Published by: R&S Publishing, Oxford, Ohio.
For more information, e-mail: rspublishing@gmail.com

THIS BOOK IS FONDLY DEDICATED
TO ALL MY STUDENTS,
NEAR AND FAR.
MAY YOU
BRIGHTEN YOUR OWN CORNER
WHEREVER YOU ARE.

Coralie Runyon Jones

Table of Contents

Preface: "Prelude" 1

Chapter 1: Childhood Memories 4
  "Cross Country Journeys"

Chapter 2: My First Year as a Teacher 12
  "What Am I Doing Here?"

Chapter 3: The Maysville Schools 23
  "Undoubted Abilities"

Chapter 4: The First Christian Church 44
  "Glory, Laud and Honor"

Chapter 5: The Civic Chorus 58
  "Singing With a Star"

Chapter 6: The Ripley Years 65
  "The Little Choir That Could"

Chapter 7: The Mason County Years: The 1960s 75
  "Building a Legacy"

Chapter 8: The Mason County Years: The Trip to England . . 87
  "The Impossible Dream"

Chapter 9: The Mason County Years: 1970-1974 101
   "Expanding Horizons"

Chapter 10: The Mason County Years: 1975-1982 117
   "Third Time's a Charm"

Chapter 11: Music at Maysville Community College 142
   "Higher Education"

Chapter 12: The Limestone Youth Orchestra 156
   "String Music"

Chapter 13: The Limestone Chorale 16
   "Play It Again"

Chapter 14: St. Michael's and St. Patrick's 183
   "Recapitulation: Students and Children of Students"

Chapter 15: A Tribute. 193
   "With A Song in Her Heart"

Coda: Appendices 197
   Developing Superior Choirs
   High School Choir Techniques
   Honors Received

Preface: "Prelude"

For a number of years I have been asked how did I do it? How could students in a small county school achieve such success in choral singing? How could they receive a superior rating year after year at contests? How could they memorize major works and astound university choral directors in Kentucky and other parts of the United States?

Many times I have been asked to write this story – a story of taking students with little musical training before entering high school and creating choirs that gave concerts in Europe and England, and being recognized as tops in choral singing. How could the choirs achieve their characteristic sound – a sound that one eminent choral conductor wanted to "bottle and sprinkle" on his college singers?

I think the answer lies in believing in the vast potential that is in each individual, in incorporating it into a whole, with the end result having a magical quality that appeals to the listener's heart. Choral conductors do not achieve that special sound by themselves – the students do it. I have always respected my young singers and believed in them. They, in turn, achieved beauty.

My teaching experience covers more than 64 years. I started in a small county high school, moved to the city school system of the county seat three miles away after one year, later taught in another school seven miles away in a neighboring state, and then completed the circle, returning to the now-consolidated schools of the county where I had started – all this within a radius of only seven miles. In the course of these six decades I started a string program that produced teachers in violin, viola, and cello; a youth symphony that attracted the support of the Kentucky Fine Arts Commission; and a community musical program that received on-going financial support from a grateful and appreciative public.

I served on the Kentucky Music Educators Board for many years, have been All-State Choral chairman and All-State Orchestra chairman, president of the Kentucky Association of String Teachers, was an adjudicator at music contests in every part of the state of Kentucky, and conducted workshops on building choruses and the teaching of strings. I have received citations from the Ohio State Legislature, the Kentucky House of Representatives, and the Kentucky Senate. My choirs were appointed Ambassadors from Kentucky to Europe and England. All of these honors enriched the music program where I taught and urged me to do it better, and to do it better, still.

Among other honors, I was selected as an Outstanding Kentucky Woman, Lady of the Year in Maysville, and the Kentucky Teacher of the Year for 1982.

The real achievement of one's life is simply to believe in yourself, to believe in your students, and to brighten the corner wherever you are, as expressed in the following old poem, whose words have always stayed with me:

Brighten Your Corner
Author unknown

We cannot all be famous
Or be listed in "Who's Who,"
But every person, great or small,
Has important work to do.

For seldom we realize
The importance of small deeds,
Or to what degree of greatness
Unnoticed kindness leads.

For it's not the big celebrity
In a world of fame and praise,
But it's doing unpretentiously
In an undistinguished way.

The work that God assigned to us
Unimportant as it seems,
That makes our task outstanding,
And brings reality to dreams.

So do not sit and idly wish
For wider, new dimensions
Where you can put into practice,
Your many good intentions.

But at the spot God placed you
Begin at once to do,
Little things to brighten up
The lives surrounding you.

preface

If everybody brightened up
The spot where they are standing,
By being more considerate,
And a little less demanding.

This dark, old world would very soon
Eclipse the evening star,
If everybody brightened up
The corner where they are!

An early piano lesson for my grandson, Ezekiel.

CHAPTER 1: CHILDHOOD MEMORIES
"Cross Country Journeys"

I was born in Bowling Green, Kentucky, on a hot Wednesday at three in the afternoon. Dr. White was the physician, and I was born at home at 1028 Elm Street. My first memories, however, were of a yellow house in Nashville, Tennessee, on the campus of Peabody College, where my father was pursuing another degree. My mother was Constance Coralie Barrington, born in Coconut Grove, Florida, and my father was Loton Brodie Jones, born in Hanson, Kentucky. He was an attorney in Bowling Green, but felt the "call" to the ministry and was getting a degree in theology at Peabody. He had five degrees in all and was a brilliant man. Mother graduated in piano at Western Normal College in Bowling Green and was a pupil of Professor Franz J. Strahm, who had been a pupil of Franz Lizst in Europe. She had absolute pitch and could play anything she had ever heard.

My next memories were of Artesia, New Mexico, where my father was minister of a Presbyterian Church there. I can still see the house in my mind's eye. We would walk down the street and around the corner to call on friends of my mother. One such friend had a very old music box that turned on a cylinder, and I remember we were always given candied grapefruit when we visited there.

There were three of us girls: Mary Bonnie, the oldest by two years, and Martha Elizabeth, the youngest by two years. One of the delights about this time in Artesia was going out to the ranch of the Hagermans – Mother's friends from the past. I remember a big pond in front of the house.

We had a Studebaker touring car – open to the elements. When it rained we had to put on the ising-glass windows. There were running boards on each side and two spare tires next to the engine – leather seats, jump seats in front of the back seats that were removed to have more room for luggage. It was a great automobile. I always sat on the left side in the back, next to the open road, and was constantly falling out. My father would stop after each discovery of my absence and back up to find me. I distinctly remember the cattle guards that I fell on quite often *chapter one*

– iron bars, instead of a gate, to keep the livestock from wandering onto the gravel roads.

We traveled all through the West on our annual return trips to Kentucky. The churches where my father was the minister would allow him the summer off to get even more education – at Columbia University and Union Theological Seminary in New York, and the University of Chicago. We would visit his mother in Kentucky and take another route back to the great West. My father was a dreadful driver, preferring the middle of the road. We always had a canvas canteen of water hanging on the top of the radiator, for service stations were few and far between. I remember seeing my first airplane – in a field in Kansas. My father stopped the car in the middle of the road and pointed to this new-fangled machine.

While in Artesia, we three girls had chicken pox. Our father had gone to Florence, Arizona, to see about a position there. We cut paper dolls out of toilet tissue and made quite a mess while we were quarantined.

We did move to Florence, and I remember arriving at the manse. As we drove up, watching a Gila monster skitter across the driveway, my mother said, "But you said there would be grass," to which my father replied, "There will be tomorrow." We went to the nursery and bought lespedeza sod (lespedeza is a curly plant of the pea family) and acquired the instant lawn my father promised. My sisters and I played around the house, especially in the dirt beside the yard of lespedeza, making roads and mud pies.

One of our first visitors in Florence was a young boy, Charles Westerman, who came riding a horse. Charles became a constant visitor and forever pestered me to give him a kiss. When we were in the first grade, I finally said, "Oh, all right. But make it quick." The teacher saw this act taking place in the cloakroom and called my father. That ended my love affair with the young cowboy.

The house seemed exciting to me with its back porch and its two small closet-like rooms at either end. In these I found a lot of beautiful rocks of all kinds, quartz in particular. Old prospectors had stored their findings in these rooms, I later learned.

The school was a brick building not far from our church; I think it was in front of it. I went to the first grade there and the second. I remember the music teacher coming in and our standing and singing songs; one of them was about the morning. The boy over the aisle playfully pulled away the seat to my desk and I fell, cutting a hole in the back of my head. I was taken to Phoenix. I remember the medicine the doctor poured into the hole, and how it burned. I still have a bump in the back of my head. My second grade teacher told my father that I was being promoted to the fourth grade, skipping the third, but that he must teach me the multiplication table. I remember standing in front of a big pot-bellied stove in the dining room and saying the tables.

We made May Day baskets and put flowers in them and hung them on neighbors' doors. We took a diagonal walk through an open block to go to school. Directly across the street lived the sister of Samuel Clemens – (Mark Twain).

We ate Sunday dinner at the Black Cat Café operated by a friendly Chinese couple. We took trips to Casa Grande, coming back through Tombstone. My father pointed out a place on the corner as the road made a sharp turn to the right. That was the scene of murders in the wild, wild West.

Constance Barrington Jones

Loton Brodie Jones

chapter one

Our next-door neighbor was a dentist named Dr. Teufort. We were invited over one night after supper to hear the great instrument he had purchased – a radio. We sat in a circle in the back room as he twisted the dials to get a station. We didn't hear much except static, but a new age was beginning.

We had a Mexican maid named Madeline, who would take us to her home when my parents were in Phoenix or Tucson. The house was built on thin stilts, and she served us hot tamales while we were there.

The Dodds lived around the corner. Dr. Maurice Dodd was the superintendent of schools in Florence, and he had two sons, Marcus and Jimmy. We played together a lot. Marcus was my beau – both of us in the second grade. Madeline performed the marriage ceremony wearing a large-fringed lampshade from the living room. Many years later, I visited the Dodds in Charleston, West Virginia, where he became supcrintendent.

One of my father's best friends was Ernest McFarland, a lawyer and member of our church. He became a U. S. Senator from Arizona. He would later visit us frequently in Bowling Green on his return trips to Arizona and took an interest in our education. Upon my graduation from Western Kentucky University, he offered me a scholarship he had obtained for me at Georgetown University in Washington, D. C., to major in political science, as well as a job in the Department

My father's church.

of Justice and the opportunity to teach private music lessons and live in their home. He was very persistent, sending telegrams and special delivery letters, but I insisted on teaching in Maysville, after one year in Orangeburg.

The trips in the summer were most interesting: Yellowstone, the Grand Canyon, the Painted Desert, the Petrified Forest, the Black Hills of South Dakota, Carlsbad Caverns in New Mexico. We stayed in hotels, as there were few motels; sometimes we stayed in tourist cabins – rustic, but equipped with kitchen facilities. We stayed in a cabin at Yellowstone, and a bear came up to the back door. At Carlsbad, while we were touring the caverns, Mother stayed in the cabin. A severe rainstorm came up and washed her violin out, but it was recovered. Blanche Hamby, a friend from Kentucky, went to Yellowstone with us. My Grandmother Palmer went west with us one summer also.

In the summertime when we came back to Kentucky, my father attended different universities for post-graduate courses in theology. He had a little library in the manse in Florence and I remember friends carting off many of the books in wheelbarrows. He had always been a bookworm. I remember Mother and Daddy destroying the Guy de Maupassant books so we girls would not read them. There were many first editions and leather-bound books; many with pages we enjoyed cutting before they could be read. Many barrels of books were sent to

Baby Coralie with her mother.

Baby Coralie with her sister, Bonnie.

Bowling Green when we returned; the basement of the State Street house was loaded with books that were given to trash men to carry off after the deaths of my parents in 1960. What a tragedy.

I remember when the movie King of Kings, directed by Cecil B. DeMille, was shown in our church. This was a very innovative thing to do in 1927. The plot was about Mary Magdalene becoming very angry when Judas, now a follower of Jesus, would not come to her feast. She goes to Jesus and becomes repentant. The showing of this movie in the church shocked many members.

My father worked with young Mexican boys and frequently took them on picnics in the desert area around Florence. I remember seeing the boys riding in the Studebaker, filling the car and hanging on to the running boards. There were no Indians in our town; they lived on the reservations and didn't join the Mexicans in their Christian Endeavor groups. Each year the church had a picnic, held in one of the dry gulleys – riverbeds with no water. We would usually stand up rather than sit down on the hot sand while we ate delicious food prepared by the women of the church.

My mother's grand piano went wherever we lived, and traveled on the train in a large wooden case. The case was our playhouse, as it rested in our backyards, ready for the next move. She gave piano lessons and had some very talented pupils, and was in demand as a professional accompanist for visiting artists. One I recall in particular was Baron Orema, Caruso's understudy. I also have a vivid memory of the time mother took me to hear Fritz Kreisler play at the University of Tucson. I was spellbound by his playing and silently decided that this was what I wanted to do. I was six years old.

I took elocution lessons from the wife of the Methodist minister. Among the pieces in my repertoire was the poem, "The Middle Child," and I would recite it at every opportunity. I had a best friend – Patty Moore.

I remember my sister Martha had long curls and there were many screams on Sunday morning when mother used the curling irons, heated on the stove, to curl her hair. Martha had a beautiful voice and at the age of four or five sang "In the Garden" in church one Sunday night, with mother playing the piano. I can remember it yet – how beautiful it was.

I also recall the time my mother's father, Edward Barrington, came to visit. We had a two-seated swing in the front yard. He was a minister and a wanderer of sorts. He held pastorates in many places: Key West, Florida; Boise, Idaho; McComb, Mississippi; Fort Myers, Florida; Bowling Green, Kentucky. As a young man he and a friend ventured into the Oklahoma Territory and escaped an unfriendly Indian encampment by calmly walking away, leaving his prized walking stick. We visited them in Idaho and in Mississippi and I remember those visits well. When we visited them in Boise, I was in a play. I had the role of a daffodil, and my grandmother, who I called Bon, made me a dress of yellow and green paper.

The sunsets in Arizona were especially beautiful. It seemed that they extended all round the firmament – brilliant colors of red, yellow, blue and green. I am grateful for the experiences we had with many wonderful friends in the churches in New Mexico and Arizona. It is a wonder we all survived the great amount of travel we did each year. Many of the roads were gravel. My father was determined that his three girls would see a great deal of America, and we did. We were a close family, and I am grateful for these early years.

A photo of me with Bonnie, right, in Florence. Our neighbor's adobe house is in the background.

chapter one

My Grandmother Palmer was always urging my father to return home and look after her interests as well as the properties he had in Bowling Green. In 1929, my father resigned his pastorate in Florence and we returned to Kentucky, taking up residence at 1028 Elm Street. Daddy had built the house for mother when they married. My grandfather had been the minister at the Cumberland Presbyterian Church from 1915 to 1918; in later years mother was the organist there, as well as Sunday School teacher. The rest of us went to the Westminster Presbyterian Church.

I remember the day Daddy bought a Dodge car and we all took a ride. I'll never forget the marvelous smell of that new car. They don't seem to have the same fragrance today.

I also remember the day I came home from school and Mother said to be very still – my father was at home. He had just lost $50,000 in the stock market crash – money my grandmother had given him to invest. It was a terrible thing! He recovered in time, but it was very sad, for us and the whole country.

The Crews, distant relatives, descended upon us. They called from the train station. Daddy went to get them and insisted they spend the night. How we all managed is interesting. To have enough beds, we had to bring in the leather seats from the Studebaker. They finally left, after a protracted visit. They made a habit of this, and mother soon was very tired of the "crew" of Crews.

Then one day Daddy purchased the house on State Street. It was big: five bedrooms, two baths, living room, dining room, and a big hall with a beautiful stairway; it came with a two-room servant house and a garage. The house had a big basement with rooms like the rooms upstairs, all filled with barrels of things, though with a dirt floor, except in the furnace room. Mandy and Mitty, a married couple, served as handyman and cook and lived in the servant house.

CHAPTER 2: MY FIRST YEAR AS A TEACHER
"What Am I Doing Here?"

On a hot day in August 1941, I stood on the corner in front of the education building of the University of Kentucky, awaiting an appointment with a man I had never met. After a long, long ride on a passenger bus, I was tired, discouraged, and somewhat afraid. A few hours earlier, I had left Bowling Green, in the southwest part of the state, where I had spent my high school and college years in the safe and secure environment of my home. I had just turned 20 the month before, and I was filled with unsettling questions.

Just a few days before, Dean Grise had called me into his office at Western Kentucky State Teachers' College to tell me that I had almost enough credits to graduate that summer. I only needed six hours to complete a bachelor of arts degree, and he asked if I wanted to see if this were possible. War was looming – many of my classmates were scattered; the boys were leaving in great numbers; the Great Depression was in full stride; the future was frightening and uncertain. I readily agreed to the dean's request, and he then called the head of the music department, Dr. John Vincent, and said, "Coralie only needs six hours to graduate. What can we do for her?" Together they decided that the six hours would somehow be accounted for and on record, and I could graduate that summer.

Dr. Grise than told me to go down the hill to the employment office and see what was available as a teaching position. An appointment was made for me to meet the superintendent of the only available school with a job opening on Western's list. Most jobs in the state had already been filled, as it was by now late in the year and school would be starting just after Labor Day. The position described to me was at the Orangeburg School in Mason County, more than 200 miles away. With some misgivings I accepted the invitation to see the school, the county, and the city of Maysville, the county seat. I never guessed that this unknown place would be where I would spend the rest of my life. Questions plagued me all the way up the curving road to Lexington. "What am I doing here? Don't I still want to be a concert violinist?" I had turned down a scholarship at the Cincinnati Conservatory of Music where I had spent the summers of 1936 and 1937 – a scholarship that would have given me three private lessons a week from Peter Froelich, my instructor at the conservatory, who insisted that I stay and pursue a professional career as a violinist. Even the president of the school urged me to accept the scholarship. My father had refused to let me do this before I received my college degree from Western. After graduating, he said I was now free to pursue my studies at the Cincinnati Conservatory. Now I was about to receive the college degree and could continue studying the violin. The question persisted: "Did I really want to teach public school music?"

After an exceedingly long wait on the corner, a car pulled up and Emory G. Rogers, the superintendent of the Mason County Schools, introduced himself and asked me to get in, and we would see the school. It was a long and hazardous journey, around more endlessly winding roads. Mr. Rogers drove very fast, for he had to show me the school and return me to Lexington so I could get back to Bowling Green. When we finally arrived in Mason County, he hurriedly drove past the Orangeburg School, waving his arm and saying: "There's the school, but you will live in town – in Maysville with the other young teachers." I did not get a real glimpse of the school on the hill where I would spend the first year of a long teaching career – over 64 years of teaching music to young students – a career what would encompass a radius of only seven miles.

Ready to take on the world – or at least Orangeburg.

After a hasty trip through picturesque Maysville on the Ohio River, Mr. Rogers explained that school would start the Tuesday after Labor Day, and I would attend a teachers' meeting the Saturday before at the Presbyterian Church in Maysville. The salary would be $76 a month for nine months, but the board of education would guarantee that I would receive a total of $85 a month by teaching private lessons in piano and violin at 50 cents a lesson. If I didn't make the needed $9, the board would supplement my salary for the $85 total. The Great Depression was still with us and the $76-$85 sounded good. I accepted the position and have never regretted doing so. All my hopes and dreams have been realized: a chance to be of service to someone else – to share my love of music with others – to have a family and rear wonderful children. All these things have been mine, and I am grateful for the training by my mother and my father, and the good advice they gave me as I began my teaching career.

Upon leaving home, my father drew up a legal contract that I eagerly signed. The contract, complete with blue paper and legal jargon, stated that first of all, my students came first. I would be kind, supportive, and teach them all that I could. Secondly, I would not turn a deaf ear to the churches that asked me to play the violin or to teach Sunday School. Thirdly, I would accept the invitations of clubs and organizations that needed my musical services. I was also told that I must tithe my income and keep a record of every penny spent. Looking back over all these years, I treasure that document.

Upon returning to Bowling Green, I graduated from Western, packed my trunk, and again took the bus to Williamstown where I visited my college friend, Dorothy Cook Taylor, for the weekend. Her father drove me to Maysville where I spent the night at the New Central Hotel, on lower Market Street. My room was tiny, in the back of the hotel, over the heating system that gurgled and shouted all night long. I couldn't sleep, wondering how I was going to manage what lay ahead. I was having second thoughts, and was truly afraid.

The next morning I attended the teachers' meeting in the Presbyterian Church and met a spirited, almost brusque young woman, Mary Lou Day. She asked me where was my luggage, for she was taking me to her home in the country, a few miles from the Orangeburg School, where I was to have room and board for the school year. Where were the young teachers I was to share lodging with in Maysville? There were none.

I spent two very lonely days at the Days' home – out in the country – no telephone to call my mother to say that I had made a great mistake and, really, should come home. I should have accepted the invitation and urging of Senator Ernest McFarland.

Many times I have daydreamed about Washington, D. C. What would my life have been like if I had gone there? But for all the supposed glamour of other places, I contented myself with pursing my career in tiny Orangeburg – not even a dot on the world's map.

The other two teachers who were also going to board at the Days' home arrived on Sunday afternoon. I could hardly wait to meet them. One of them had a car! They were young! We'd have a good time together! I soon noticed that the two did not talk to me directly or answer any questions. We were to share a bedroom in the upstairs of the Days' home – the attic. I had a single bed, but they shared a double bed. One had a radio and after retiring for the night, I remarked that the radio was playing my favorite song: "I Don't Want To Set the World on Fire." Immediately, the owner of the radio turned it down to a very faint sound and remarked, "I wish we had earphones so we could listen – and no one else." I then realized that I was an outsider and not wanted but didn't know what I had done to cause such animosity. My hostess,

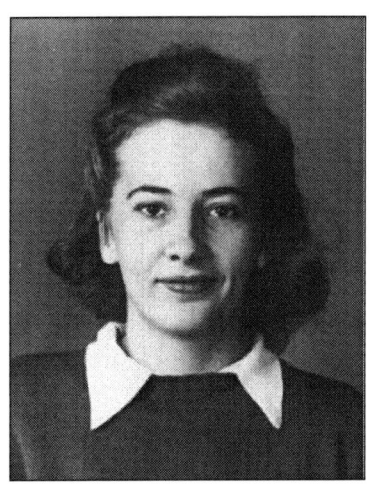

Mary Lou, had come upstairs and was standing at the foot of my bed. She tweaked my toe. I can distinctly remember this act of kindness – or so it seemed to me.

The next day was a very lonely one. The two teachers took off in the CAR, and I was left to my own devices. I yearned for a telephone to call my mother. This was not going to work at all! I wanted to go home! Mary Lou said she was moving me into my own room – a tiny room, not quite finished and smelling very strongly of varnish – but mine, alone! The bathroom was down the stairs, and I had to go through the bedroom of Mary Lou and Phil to get to it – but it all worked out. I can still see and feel that room. It was unbearably hot on the warm days of the fall, and the odor of fresh paint and varnish were overwhelming, but I was glad to have my own space.

Tuesday finally dawned. After breakfast – silently partaken of – the two teachers left in the CAR. Phil had already gone to work, and I was left to get to school, which was several miles away, the best I could. So I walked. When I reached downtown Orangeburg, which consisted of a church and a general store, I was stopped by a young lady in a Model T Ford. She was a teacher and asked if I wanted a ride. I gratefully rode the rest of the way, up a gravelly road, to the school on top of a hill. I made friends with the second-grade teacher, "Blue" Voiers, who lived in Tollesboro, a few miles away. She passed by the Days' home, and she offered to pick my up each day. I paid her $6 a month for this transportation, and we became very close friends. This cut into my take-home pay quite a bit – with retirement taken out, room and board at $1 a day and the tithe, little was left. I managed, however, and found a store in Maysville, Henley's, where I could purchase wonderful dresses for $25. I had to pay for them a little each month, but Mr. Rosenthal, the owner, and I became good friends, and he was kind to extend credit.

I had a homeroom with 13 students for whom I had to keep records of attendance in the famous – or infamous – "Bird Book." (so named because of the cardinal on the cover). I never could keep it straight. At the end of the year my principal, Robert R. Martin, a large, brilliant man, who later became the state superintendent of public instruction and later still the president of Eastern Sate University, kept it at the end of the school year to straighten it out. I did not get my final check until late in August, for he had a difficult time with the mess I had made of it.

I noticed at once that first day of school that one of my former roommates was the home economics teacher, whose room was just across the hall. Word soon got out in Orangeburg and the educational provinces of Mason County that things were not pleasant with some of the faculty. I was surprised a few days later to have the superintendent, Mr. Rogers, and the board of education members visit my classes. I was asked to attend a conference with the superintendent in his office in downtown Maysville. We had to go into town each month to this quaint building on the corner of Third and Sutton Streets to receive our paychecks. We had to raise our right hand and swear that we had not fought a duel. The office was up a narrow flight of steps and was quite tiny. Mr. Rogers, assuming I was very unhappy and would give up my job and return to my home in Bowling Green, insisted I give it some time before I made my decision. He was anxious for me to stay, for he was a musician, too, and played the violin! In later years he gave me some of his violin music, which I still have.

I knew I didn't want to be a quitter. I'd have to make the best of it. A few days later, the teacher across the hall came to my room, knocked on my door, and said how sorry she was for her actions. She explained that the two of them had cooked up a plan in that summer to run off any teacher that was be hired to replace the one they had before. It was the policy of the board of education to try to get a qualified teacher for music, and failing to do so, they would employ a part-time teacher, who was Mary Lou Day! Such was the auspicious beginning of a teaching career that would last 64 years and is still going strong!

My duties consisted of teaching music in grades 1-6, the 7th and 8th grade chorus, the high school chorus, 9th grade English, and high school Civics. I was also asked to coach the cheerleaders. Since I had never attended a basketball game, even at Ed Diddle's Western – I was too busy practicing – I knew no cheers but perhaps: "Rah, rah, rah, Orangeburg, Orangeburg!" I knew no fancy routines, and advised the cheerleaders to scoop up their hands as they said each "rah" and to shake their pompoms! We managed. I had to ride on the rickety yellow school bus of 1930s vintage and attend all the games.

One game has always stood out in my mind – a home game against the powerhouse, Maysville. Orangeburg won that game! The coach was Earle D. Jones, and many years later, after the death of my husband, Harold E. Runyon, we were married. The Orangeburg win was such a triumph that school was dismissed the following day, and the faculty had lunch in Maysville at Caproni's on the river – a quaint and popular restaurant where you could order their famous spaghetti dinner for 50 cents – each meatball was 10 cents extra.

On my basketball trips chaperoning the cheerleaders, I noticed that several different local men would ride the school bus, too. They would ask me if I would like to walk with them. This was a considered date. I refused them all.

I was soon invited to play the violin in Maysville – a metropolis compared to Orangeburg – especially at the First Baptist Church where Dr. Odom, a lawyer-turned minister, was the pastor. We became good friends, and I played at his church many times. It was he who wrote the Maysville school board, and I still have the letter, suggesting that they attend a concert at the Orangeburg School – which they did, sitting in a row in our gymnasium-auditorium – and later asking me to teach in the Maysville Schools.

Mary Lou, my landlady, was an accomplished pianist, having studied at the University of Louisville, and she became my accompanist for the year I was at Orangeburg. We performed at many of the churches in the area, and it was great fun to play at small country churches. This was my first experience at churches in the "wildwood," and I thoroughly enjoyed it. Mary Lou gave piano lessons, and many times I heard her call out a mistake when she was in the kitchen preparing the evening meal.

I'll never forget the experience of eating lunch in the school's basement lunchroom. The cook was a kindly soul, but one of the most unfortunate, homely persons I had ever seen. She was painfully thin and had a hooked nose with a large wart on the tip of it. We ate on tin plates, and the usual fare was scrambled eggs made of a powdered substance of government surplus. It took a bit of doing to endure these repasts. The cost was 10 cents a meal.

One of my violin pupils arrived at school one afternoon with a violin he had secured from his grandfather and said he wanted to study, but there was a problem. The cost of the lesson was 50 cents, and he had only a quarter and no possible way of getting any more. I told him that was not a problem: just get another student to share the lesson with him, and we would proceed upon his musical education.

I had no inkling what the year of violin instruction would mean to the young boy, Richard Zeigler, or what it would mean to me several years later. Richard went on to college, was successful in the business world and still remembered his experiences with music lessons on the violin. He wanted to repay his old teacher and did so with the founding of the Coralie Runyon-Jones Music Library. This generous gift provides a place for lovers of classical music to enjoy listening to and reading about music of the ages. A wing in the Mason County Public Library was set aside and opened in the spring of 2005.

Another pupil of violin, Harriet Halfhill, did so well that her parents purchased an excellent violin for her, and I remember with fondness the trip we made to Cincinnati to choose the right instrument. Her sister, Josephine, studied voice with me, and I was thrilled to find that she had the potential of becoming a fine coloratura soprano. She followed me to Maysville, continued her lessons, and was a valued member of my choral groups there. I urged her to study at the Cincinnati Conservatory of Music, which she did. She was also a valued member of my church choir in Maysville, and in her annual letter at Christmas, she has told me how much she misses the wonderful experiences at Orangeburg and Maysville.

One afternoon, I was asked by a young man from neighboring Vanceburg to have a Sunday ride, and about 3 p.m. we heard the announcement that Pearl Harbor had been attacked.

It was December 7, 1941.

The next morning our principal called all the students and teachers to come to the library, find a seat, even on the floor, and listen to President Roosevelt announce that the Japanese had attacked the United States and we were at war. Rationing began, and the residents would come to the school to receive their ration coupons allowing them to have shoes, bread, gasoline, and other restricted items. Robert R.

Martin had a B sticker for gasoline that allowed him to move about more readily than others. He often asked me to accompany him into the city on nightly treks to chat with the editor of the Daily Independent, Martha Comer. I thoroughly enjoyed sitting in the corner of the second floor newspaper room listening to these two very wise people talking about the events of the day and the status of the world. Martha and I became very dear friends in later years, and I, too, loved to go to the office of the Daily Independent and talk to her. As I continued my teaching career in Maysville, Ripley, and later Mason County, she was an enthusiastic supporter of mine and wrote enthusiastic articles about the concerts I gave. She and I enjoyed playing bridge together, and she lived a long and meaningful life, and I miss her very much.

    I worked hard to develop good choruses at the Orangeburg School and decided to take the junior high chorus to the music contest in Lexington in the spring of 1942. Mr. Martin, the principal, and the accompanist, Anna Mac Cox, who taught at another school in the county, accompanied us, and we eagerly but fearfully arrived at the University of Kentucky in Lexington for our first contest experience. To our amazement and chagrin we found that we had come a day late. The contest for choruses had already taken place. However, the head of the music department of the university, Mildred Lewis, arranged for us to perform and we did so before the judges for the solos and ensembles scheduled for the second day of the festival. One of the two selections was Mozart's "Cradle Song," and we earned the rating of superior. That was the first top rating to be earned by the hundreds of entries in the years to come, and it was then that I decided that only the very best was good enough for my students.

    The senior class of 1942 had planned a trip to Cumberland Falls, but her physician told the class sponsor, Lula Calvert Wood, that she was not physically able to chaperone the trip. The principal asked me to take her place, and I agreed even though I was reluctant to do so. The trip would be after school was dismissed for the summer, and I wanted to go home to Bowling Green. However, we set off in an almost dilapidated school bus for a trip I will never forget. We slowly made our way down the winding roads and made a stop at some small service station for repairs to the bus. It had grown quite dark by now, and after the bus was repaired enough to continue, Mr. Martin, who had accompanied us as another chaperone, called the roll and found two boys missing. After a frantic search, the fun-loving ones were found, somewhat worse for wear.

We proceeded to our destination, one of the new state parks in Kentucky at Cumberland Falls. By this time it was quite dark, and rain had begun to fall. When we arrived, hoping for a nice cottage with clean sheets, bath and towels and soap, I found to my amazement that the girls would sleep on the bus, while the boys would make do on a concrete slab outside. This next morning the girls and I occupied a primitive cabin with damp and clammy sheets on damp and clammy bunks. We survived the night, and Mr. Martin announced that breakfast was ready – his treat for us. The menu consisted of cold pork and beans served outside the bus – we had no other place. After breakfast, he asked me if I would like to see the rainbow behind Cumberland Falls. On the walk he pointed out the builders working on Dupont Lodge, which would replace the cabins, which had no bathroom facilities. In later years, my family and I visited Cumberland Falls and enjoyed the beautiful Dupont Lodge.

However, the principal and I arrived at the scenic wonder, walked down the steep, winding, rain-soaked steps leading to the area behind the falls and there we viewed the rainbow. I was very surprised when Robert turned to me and asked me to marry him! We had not had dated other than the occasional trip to talk to Martha Comer. He was insistent, and I was just as insistent that this was out of the question. I told him I had other things to do – teach in Maysville, and then go to Arizona to teach. I told him I had great ambitions, and I had a long way to go. He assured me that he would get to the top before I did. He realized his dream when he later became president of Eastern State University. He visited me several times after he joined the Army and was on leave from his duties in weather forecasting, stationed in Alaska. He always asked me the same question, and I always gave the same answer. In the summer after the great trip to Cumberland Falls with the graduates of 1942, he called for me nearly every day while I was in Bowling Green attending graduate school at Western. My father seemed to answer the phone each time he called. When finally I talked to him and he asked what I was doing, I responded that I was reading Guizot's *History of France* – books my father had in the upstairs library that I had never opened. The library had high ceilings like the rest of the house and the walls were lined with deep tomes. After finally realizing he was rejected, Robert R. Martin went on to lead a full and happy life. He died a few years ago.

Commencement exercises for the Orangeburg High School were held May 28, 1942 at 8:30 p.m., Central War Time. The program follows:

    Processional – "Tannhauser March," by Wagner
    Invocation: Rev. O. S. Crain
    "I Love Life," by Mana-Zucca: High School Chorus
    Andante from Violin Concerto in D, by Wieneswski:
        Miss Coralie Jones
    Presentation of Speaker: Robert R. Martin, Principal
    Wartime Tasks of Our Schools: Hon. John W. Booker
    Presentation of Diplomas: Emory G. Rogers, Superintendent
        of Schools
    "To Thee, O Country," by Eichberg: High School Chorus
    Benediction: Rev. Bayard McCann
    Recessional: "War March of the Priests," by Mendelssohn

Chapter 3: The Maysville Schools
"Undoubted Abilities"

On March 27, 1942, Dr. A. D. Odom, minister of the First Baptist Church in Maysville, sent a letter to Mr. Louis Laukhuf, superintendent of the Maysville Schools, on my behalf:

Dear Mr. Laukhuf:

It has recently come to my attention that Miss Priest will not submit an application for reemployment with the city school system for next year. I have been very much impressed with the personality and ability of Miss Coralie Jones, now with the Orangeburg School.

I believe that it would greatly advantage your board to check on her availability. I am somehow persuaded that a larger field of activity will seek her undoubted abilities.

This is merely a suggestion from one interested in this work.

In June 1942, Rev. Robert von Thurn, minister of the First Presbyterian Church, Maysville, wrote:

To Whom It May Concern:

It is a pleasure to make a statement as to the character of Miss Coralie Jones. It has been my good fortune to know Miss Jones as a musician of fine ability, as a frequent guest in our home, and as a friend. She has the unusual knack of leading out children to do their very best, and of winning their affection at the same time. In this community in which Miss Jones has taught during the past school year, she has made a wide circle of friends. Her generosity in giving time to render violin solos, repeatedly, for church after church, has become well known. Miss Jones has a happy, cheerful disposition that will make friends wherever she goes. I can heartily commend Miss Jones to anyone needing her unusual abilities.

The Public Ledger, in reporting the board meeting of the city schools held in the summer: "Miss Coralie Jones, of Bowling Green, was elected music supervisor to replace Miss Mary E. Priest, who will be married this month. Miss Jones is well known to the people of Maysville, having taught this past year at Orangeburg. It will be recalled that she was the only music teacher in Mason County who received a superior rating at the music festival in Lexington. Miss Jones is an accomplished violinist and has played on numerous occasions in Maysville churches. She has an exceptional musical background and very definitely a winning way with children. Miss Jones did her undergraduate work in Western State Teacher's College and also has two summers' work at the Conservatory of Music in Cincinnati."

During the summer of 1942, after I agreed to teach in Maysville, I received several interesting telephone calls. One was from Rev. Hilton Windley, the minister of the First Christian Church in Maysville, who invited me to be the choir director of that church. I accepted. Another was from Rev. Robert von Thurn, the minister of the First Presbyterian Church, asking me to room with his family at the parsonage. I also agreed to that request. He also asked me to work with the music of the church, but since I had already agreed to be the choir director of First Christian, he asked if I would play for the Sunday School assembly on Sunday mornings. I enjoyed doing that and then walking down the block and a half to the other church for my choir duties.

When I arrived at the von Thurns, I found that I was to share a room with one of my students, Anne, their daughter. Each night I had a stack of elementary music texts to study and prepare for the next day's teaching. Mrs. von Thurn told me how glad she was that I was rooming with them, for the $15 a month I would be paying for room and board would be placed in the sugar bowl hidden in the Dutch cupboard in the kitchen. Into the bowl went the honorariums Dr. von Thurn received for weddings and funerals; the von Thurns were saving up for Anne to go to Wellesley. They also purchased a side of veal, since I was eating breakfast and dinner with them.

In just a few weeks I was urged to move to 227 Sutton Street where two other teachers in the Maysville schools roomed. This was a beautiful home called "Phillip's Folly" (also known as "Fee's Folly") and it was rumored to have been both a slave pen for the imprisonment of recaptured fugitive slaves – under its original owner, the mayor of the city who built it in 1831 – and later, under a subsequent owner, a station on the underground railroad. Chains in the cellar bear witness to its original use.

I screwed up my courage to tell the von Thurns that I wanted to move and they reminded me that I had dashed their hopes for Anne to go to Wellesley. I felt very sad at this predicament, but it was the best thing to do since I had no car, and the schools were too scattered and far away for walking. My new home on Sutton Street was just three blocks from the high school. I was given the back room on the second floor. It was a beautiful room, furnished in antiques. I was happy with my two housemates, Elaine Smith and Nancy Botts. We were young and happy together in Mrs. Darlington Fee's beautiful home. When Mrs. Fee was in Florida for the winter, Miss Lutie Collins took charge of chaperoning us. The arrangement worked perfectly for me and I was later glad to find out that Anne von Thurn did go to Wellesley in spite of my defection.

I was very excited to teach in Maysville. The Orangeburg year had given me self-confidence, and I was eager to go on and create a strong choral program. Maysville was close to Cincinnati, and I could attend the symphony, opera, and ballet concerts there. The trip on the train just took an hour, and many of us would take the 6 a.m. train, eat breakfast in the diner, take a cab from Covington to downtown Cincinnati, eat lunch at the Netherland Plaza Hotel and watch the ice-skating show, shop, go to the Willis Music store for supplies, and take the train back to Maysville, returning at 6 p.m.

It was wonderful to live at 227 Sutton Street. I ate three meals a day at the fabulous Harbeson. Mrs. Nan Harbeson, a wonderful cook, owned this "boarding house". She used Spode and Haviland china, sterling silver, and beautiful linens for her guests. She had a few permanent boarders. Mr. And Mrs. Tune lived upstairs in her home and owned a dress shop. Several teachers were allowed to have their meals there, and we sat at a round table in the dining room. We ate delicious rolls, corn pudding, country ham, broiled chicken, Kentucky bourbon cake, homemade ice cream, transparent puddings, and many other delicious Mason County examples of gourmet dining, or we would be in grave dispute with Mrs. Harbeson. All of this for $30 a month! When we felt that we needed a break from such delicious but fattening food, we would sneak across the street to the Kilgus Drug Store for one of their marvelous sandwiches and a coke. We even, occasionally, slipped into Traxel's Restaurant on Second Street for a quick supper including dessert for just 50 cents. The restaurant had a party room upstairs, where many of our children's birthday parties were held later with cake and ice cream in a variety of molds. This slipping away for the Harbeson was not looked upon with favor by the chef and owner. We were quite frightened and in awe of Nan Harbeson. She would receive our monthly payment for which she deducted the times we were away with an exceedingly gruff manner, saying, "What a pittance!" as she snatched the check out of our hands. But, for some reason, possibly my position of teaching music and having many of my students performing at banquets in her formal dining rooms, Mrs. Harbeson was nice to me. She taught a Sunday School class at First Christian, just across the street from her home, and as I was the director of music there, she showed favoritism to me. I am very grateful for the wonderful experience of eating at the Harbeson. We all learned a lot about the gracious art of dining and entertaining.

 I had a wonderful music room at the high school. It was large and had a fireplace. This was not used, of course, but it was attractive with a mantel and mirror. I had a small red piano in the room and a tiny office. Outside the office window was a round fire escape shaped like a silo. It went to the top of the building, and the boys were allowed to use it during fire drills. The girls used the stairs, as did the teachers.

 I had a large chorus and I was surprised to notice that the back row contained many six-foot tall boys. These young men, stars on the basketball team, had enrolled in chorus to give the teacher a hard time. In just a few days I had thrown them out. Years later, one of the expelled ones, Elza Whalen, was my formidable principal at the new Mason County High School where I taught beginning in 1960. Most of the teachers were very afraid of him. He was stern and wore a long, long face. He informed me one day that I had thrown him out of chorus, back in 1942. I became very fond of Elza Whalen, my erstwhile student, and together we planned great things for my choral students. He is one of the best bridge players in Maysville, and I have enjoyed playing against him at the Duplicate Bridge Club.

 There were four elementary schools in Maysville: First District, Center, Forest Avenue, and Sixth Ward Schools. I taught in all of them and rode the city bus to each. The fare was 10 cents, and I was reimbursed at the end of each month for my transportation. I accepted the job in Maysville for $90 a month for the nine months, but the superintendent called me within a few weeks to tell me they were increasing my salary to $100 monthly. I was told that I must not let any of the other teachers know about the raise. I loved the teachers in each of these schools. They were supportive of music and helped me in many, many ways. At the Sixth Ward School, the custodian, Mr. Frost, loved music. He had been an end man in a minstrel group that performed on one of the passenger boats that plied the Ohio River. He often stood in the door to watch me teach the young students. Once in a while he would play ragtime music on an old beat-up upright piano in the basement of the school.

I was surprised to see a strange man crammed into one of the desks in the fourth-grade room at the Center School. I whispered to the classroom teacher, Rhetta Byar, "What's going on?" She replied that she had a new pupil, Mr. Nicholas, the owner of a restaurant on Market Street. He was attending classes so he could learn to speak English. Like many of his kin, he had come to Maysville from Greece to seek his fortune. It was a fun experience to teach songs to young high-pitched voices with a deep bass joining in. He learned much from these young boys and girls and made a success in his many enterprises in the days to come.

Miss Edith Davis was the principal of the Forest Avenue School and we had a fine time there. She brought country ham on homemade biscuits, transparent puddings, and other delicacies in a linen-covered basket to school to give the teachers a treat. I also enjoyed many luncheons in her home prepared by her sister Mary. They were also vintners and made wine in their cellar. Miss Davis would call in her best friends to stomp on the grapes in a large tub in this winemaking process, and gave a sample of her exceedingly potent product to privileged ones on rare occasions. The two sisters lived in an ancient house in the county and told me the bricks had been made by hand on the site. The home was furnished with priceless antiques. Miss Mary showed me the gorgeous quilts she had made. I especially remember the Lafayette Plume pattern that she had done, one of her most prized quilts. It took a special navy blue percale with tiny white dots in it, and the material was hard to find.

Miss Lyle Hutchison was the second grade teacher at the First District School, and she was one of the finest teachers I have ever met. When she celebrated her 50th anniversary of teaching, a friend, Maida Verville, and I arranged a party for her in the classroom. It was a meaningful occasion for one who had devoted all of her life to teaching. She was also one of the most loyal and helpful members of the First Christian Church. She was a great help to me when I developed a multiple choir program there and was a great influence on many people. She spent endless hours tutoring young people in the church after school when she retired from the public schools.

One of the reasons I was looking forward to teaching in the Maysville Schools came when I was helping one of my good accompanists, Ruth Manning. She had played for me when I gave violin performances at Orangeburg, and we continued playing together when I taught in Maysville. She was from North Carolina and had come to Maysville as a bride when she married Stephen Manning. She was an excellent pianist and could handle the difficult accompaniments for my violin solos. She had a lovely home, a Steinway grand piano, and we had some wonderful times together. She was the organist-choir director of the South Methodist Church and once asked me to help with a cantata she wanted to do at Easter. While working with the musicians, I met a young man with a gorgeous voice, Tom Keith. I realized he possessed a tremendous boy soprano voice, and I was anxious to work with him in the schools. He was in the 8th grade at this time. By fall his voice had changed and he had a beautiful baritone voice. I accompanied him at many clubs and programs. Tom later studied at the College of Music in Cincinnati while he was still in high school. He later became a doctor with a practice in Cincinnati. While attending the Harvard Medical School, he was a soloist in a cathedral in Boston. Tom Keith was one of the most talented students I have ever had the pleasure to teach.

I had many outstanding and talented students those years in Maysville: Jane Russell with a gorgeous soprano voice who later attended the Eastman School of Music in Rochester, New York; Peggy Parker, a marvelous alto; Mary Milton Russell, an outstanding soprano with absolute pitch; Marion Russell, with a voice that should have been trained for operatic work; Orin Simmerman, a minister's son with a marvelous bass voice; Leslie Parry, a budding coloratura soprano; Josephine Halfhill, another coloratura soprano; Helen Nicholas, a lovely soprano; Glenn Mattingly, Donald Wood, Lida Crockett and on an on – so many beautiful voices.

In my first year of teaching at Maysville I presented the pageant that is done annually at the Church of Bartholomew in New York City, "The Pageant of the Holy Nativity," arranged by Leonard Young and Daniel McWilliams. I had found a copy in Cincinnati during one of my music explorations at the Willis Music Company. I had the chorus to process up the narrow, winding steps to the balcony in the Maysville High School auditorium where they sang while the pageant was being enacted on a beautifully lit stage. Hootie Gilbert, the custodian of the school, reminded me for the rest of my tenure in the Maysville school system that moving the little red piano from my classroom to the balcony was been a Herculean task. Mr. Gilbert was a wonderful helpmate for me. When I insisted that the chorus have risers, and the school was not able to purchase them, he made the risers himself, and they were used to good effect in the pageant.

The chorus opened the concert with "Now Let Every Tongue Adore Thee" by Bach, followed by "Lo, How A Rose E'er Blooming" by Praetorius, Tchaikovsky's "Legend" and "I Wonder As I Wander," arranged by John Jacob Niles with Jane Russell, soloist. After Joseph Clokey's "Snow Legend" and Kountz's "The Sleigh," the chorus made its way to the balcony singing "O, Come, All Ye Faithful." In the pageant, the choir sang the Aracadelt "Ave Maria," the "Hail, Mary" with Glenn Mattingly, tenor, and "The Magnificat" with Jane Russell, soprano, and Tom Keith, flute; "There Were Shepherds" with Betty Morgan, soprano, followed. After "Glory to God" by the chorus, Tom Keith presented "Let Us Now Go to Bethlehem," and the chorus replied with "Oh, I Would Go To Bethlehem" and "We Three Kings of Orient Are." Martha Logdson was the soprano soloist in "O Holy Night" and the chorus concluded the program with "Silent Night." The choir members for this first memorable Christmas concert were Betty Anderson, Katherine Atherton, Betty Ruth Breeze, Katherine Burke, Donna Mae Bright, Marjorie Cantrill, Marie Cantrill, Jeanne Caproni, Lida Crockett, Joyce Davis, Dorothy Elrod, Anna Pearl Fowler,

Norma Jean Ginn, Laura Mae Grigson, Jewell Groce, Margie Howe, Nina Kalb, Enola Kurtz, Gay Lambert, Martha Logsdon, Jane Lloyd, Dorothy Marshall, Wilma McClure, Betty Morgan, Martha Myers, Helen Nicholas, Mary Nicholas, Charlotte Newell, Peggy Parker, Leslie Parry, Dorothy Phillips, Wilma Rankin, Mary Milton Russell, Mary Julia Samuel, Carolyn Schmidt, June Staker, Betty Stevenson, Ann von Thurn, Pauline Todd, Mildred Turnipseed, Ann Gordon Wallingford, Charles Bramble, Tom Keith, Ronald LeForge, James Likins, Glen Mattingly, Joe Newell, Gaylord Roger, Ted Whaley, and Donald Wood.

The public loved the program, and accolades and honors followed. I realized at this early stage of my life that success breeds success. One must have imagination, knowledge, and a tremendous desire for the students to achieve and succeed. My father was correct in telling me my students came first. I have tried to instill in the many student teachers that came to me in later years that first of all, one must have the knowledge and training necessary and secondly, one must have imagination and a desire for perfection that cannot be quenched.

World War II was raging in Europe, and the local papers were full of reports of the numerous inductees. New ration books were available in the city schools. The first air raid test was called in October 1942. The school children engaged in a collection drive called the Key Kollection Kampaign with 13,243 keys given by the city children. Betty Stevenson, a 10th grader, accounted for 362, the highest number turned in by any pupil in the school system. June Staker, another 10th grader, was second with 339. The elementary pupil contributing the greatest number of keys in each room of various buildings received a cash reward of $1.00 donated by the January and Wood Company, and in Junior and Senior High, each school was rewarded with the same amount. A scrap metal drive was conducted, and homeowners gave iron railings and other metal objects. The local War Price and Rationing Board, composed of J. C. Everett, chairman, R. G. Utter, and H. M. Walker, granted applications for new tires and recaps for passenger cars and trucks. Women could no longer purchase nylon hose and Merz Brothers put a large ad in the local papers saying:

"We do not have a pair of nylon stockings in our entire stock

– nor do we have even one pair on order… We are not hoarding nylon hose. We are not in sympathy with any wholesaler or retailer who is. We have plenty of beautiful hose in rayon and lisle! which for all purposes are so much prettier and lovelier than you ever dreamed they could be made… priced in strict accordance with O.O.P.A. regulations.79 cents to $1.45."

Citizens were urged to help the war effort in many ways. An editorial appearing in the Public Ledger urged the public to:

Get in the Scrap

"Get in the scrap" is the rallying cry of the Mason County Farm Bureau, which is behind a movement here to collect metal for America's war effort. Every person taking part in the salvage drive will help furnish defense factories with the material to manufacture cannons, shells, and cartridges.

The Farm Bureau Committee behind the Mason County metal collection is appealing to every household to make discarded pots, pans, old stoves, broken knives, trowels, sickles, hoe blades, etc. available for the materials of war. These articles are not being bagged – 50 cents per hundredweight is being paid for the metal. "Get Into the Scrap!"

The public was urged to buy war bonds and stamps. A notice appeared in the Public Ledger that "the pin boys of Johnny Clarke's duck pin alley, all 20 of them, have joined the payroll deduction plan for the purchase of War Saving Stamps and Bonds and with an average commitment of 100 percent. Fine work, boys. Thirty-four nurses at Hayswood Hospital reported 100 percent participation in their bond-buying program and have increased their deduction percentage to 7 percent plus." The Modern Laundry and Dry Cleaning Company ran an ad: "Help win the war – free war stamps with every $1.00 worth of laundry and dry cleaning brought to our plant and called for. Will you help with the war? Save two ways--with war stamps and eliminating delivering costs."

Sugar Rationing

It was announced by Leon Henderson, Price Administrator, that under the impending sugar rationing program, hoarders will face stiff penalties – as much as ten years in prison – and a $10,000 fine for falsifying statements on the amount of the staple they have on hand. The first ration books to be issued since the war began will be distributed to every man, woman, and child in the nation. Each book will contain 26 stamps to cover purchases over eight-week periods. They will be issued through the nation's public schools, where at least one member of each household must register. The registrant will be requested to register for other members of his or her family. The amount of sugar each person will be permitted to buy a week will probably be twelve ounces.

Further rationing included automobile tires. It was reported that "Dr. W. M. Savage, local physician, was granted permission to purchase tires and tubes for his car.. Only four passenger car tires per week will be rationed locally."

In January 1942, Miss Lillie Rae Pecor, librarian, accepted the responsibility of local director for the "Victory Book Campaign," a nationwide effort to collect books for men in the armed forces in the United States.

Maysville High School was on the corner of Second and Limestone Streets. Students were allowed to walk down a block or so for lunch at Rex Parker's Drug Store, the Elite Café, and the White Light Hamburger stand at Third and Limestone. Other businesses on Second Street were: Henley's Dress shop, Tune's, Vance's Drug Store, Duck Pin Bowling Alley, the Singer Sewing Machine Company, C. L. Mains and Son Furniture Store, Hendrickson's Paint and Wallpaper Store, Caproni's Grocery, the State National Bank, the Bank of Maysville, and the Security Bank. Wood's Drug Store was on the corner of Second and Market and had an interesting circular iron stairway in the back of the store.

In December 1942, I directed an operetta entitled, "The Maid and the Golden Slipper." Ella Mae Quertermous, the third grade teacher at the Forest Avenue School, assisted me along with the sixth grade students of Miss Edith Davis. Ruth Manning provided the piano accompaniment. Dawn Grabill waa cast as Cinderella, who was left at home after her two jealous sisters, June Harover and Jean Osborne, set off for the ball. Ray Davis portrayed the fairy godmother that magically changed Cinderella's rags to a beautiful gown of yellow and gave her golden slippers so that she, too, might dance at the palace. Sammy Traughber was the prince who was under the spell of Cupid, (Nicky Nicholas), and fell in love with Cinderella. Betty Whelan enacted the role of the wicked stepmother. The presentation drew a large crowd of parents and friends of the 50 pupils in the presentation.

In the fall of 1942 the superintendent, Louis Laukhuf, called me in to discuss the band program at the school. He asked me if I could recommend someone to take over this position. I replied that I knew one of the very best: John K. Farris, of Bowling Green. I had gone to college with him and knew that he was proficient on every instrument in the band, as well as on violin and cello. Mr. Laukhuf called him, but Johnny was not available until the next school year. Whereupon Mr. Laukhuf asked me if I would take over the band duties in the high school in addition to my choral duties. I agreed and directed the band until the position was filled by John Farris in the fall of 1943. Mr. Farris soon distinguished himself and was considered one of the most outstanding directors in the state. His students received the rating of superior year after year and he stayed in the Maysville schools until his retirement.

I enjoyed working with the band, for the students were talented and a pleasure to teach. On warm days the band practiced marching down the streets with a host of majorettes, flag bearers and band sponsors. The band also played at the basketball games and performed at halftime. The best I could do was have them form a big M facing one side – then turn around and form the M for the other side of the gymnasium!

In my teaching career I have become convinced that in every situation there are a host of talented students. It is the job of the teacher to find these students, fan the flame of talent that is in them, and rejoice with them in their accomplishments. I found a great number of talented young people as soon as I began teaching in the Maysville schools. I was asked constantly to supply musical programs for various groups in the city. The Public Ledger in the fall of 1942 reported on such a program:

"Maysville's popular duo, Miss Jane Russell and Miss Peggy Parker, presented three delightful selections yesterday afternoon before the membership of the Younger Women's Club at their regular luncheon-session at the Harbeson. Accompanied at the piano by Miss Coralie Jones, music instructor in the city schools, the two high school students sang 'If I Could Tell You,' 'This Is Worth Fighting For,' and 'When the Lights Go On Again.' A most enjoyable part of the program was the violin solo rendered by Miss Jones, Kreisler's 'The Old Refrain.' Her accompanist at the piano was Mrs. Stephen Manning."

Another student who appeared frequently on programs in the community was Tom Keith. Various quartets and trios appeared frequently with Jane Russell, Mary Milton Russell, Leslie Parry, Jewell Groce, Peggy Parker, Donnie Wood, John Cochran, Orin Simmerman, Lida Crockett, and Tom Keith.

Since I was the band director at the high school I was asked to play in the Maysville Civic Band, directed by Clarence Moore. I decided that this was a good way to meet one of the young men who was dating Nancy Botts, our popular housemate. I asked Harold Runyon, a young optometrist, if I could borrow his clarinet to use in the band. He was very kind to lend me his Selmer, a silver instrument. I never took it out of its case, as I had no intention of playing in the band. (I couldn't play the clarinet.) Instead, we became good friends, had many wonderful times together bowling at the duck-pin alley, seeing movies at the Russell Theater, having dinner at Traxel's, and visiting his parents in nearby Ewing, in Fleming county. We became engaged at Easter, and my mother visited Maysville to meet Harold and his parents.

We were married in June and had a wonderful life together. We were married for 32 years before he died after a short illness. We had two wonderful children, Randolph Paul and Constance Coralie. Both children were musical and did well in school. Connie studied piano and flute in Cincinnati and Randy studied piano, flute, and pipe organ in Cincinnati. Connie received her AB degree from the University of Kentucky and her MA and doctorate in music education from Indiana University and is professor of music at the Owensboro Technical and Community College. Randy attended Harvard University, St. John's College, and Johns Hopkins University, and received the Ph.D. degree from Hopkins. He is professor of French at Miami University in Oxford, Ohio, and the author of many books and articles in his field of French literature and literary criticism. Both of my children have held church positions for many years. Randy is currently choirmaster and organist for a Lutheran church in Hamilton, Ohio. Connie has conducted national choruses in Dallas and Albuquerque, and is the national president of the Association of Disciple Musicians. She has been choir director at a First Christian Church in Owensboro for many years. My children also have blessed me with four wonderful grandchildren, Catherine and Hillary Ford and Ezekiel and Augusta Runyon.

Dr. and Mrs. Harold Runyon, 1943.

Dr. E.T. Runyon, Minnie Runyon, Constance B. Jones, L.B. Jones.

It was indeed a wonderful day when I asked Harold Runyon if I could borrow his clarinet.

In May 1943, Elaine Smith and Nancy Botts gave a beautiful linen and crystal shower for me in the rose gardens of the Fee House where we all three resided. The guests included Mrs. Louis H. C. Laukhuf, Nancy Kidwell, Catherine Patterson, Lucy Woodruff, Mildred Gravette, Edith Davis, Mabel Dye, Verna Ellis, Ella Mae Quertermous, Hazel Wells, Elizabeth Bullock, Ruth Manning, and Mrs. Martin Voiers.

The baccalaureate service for the 42 graduates of Maysville High School was held June 13, 1943, with Dr. Henry Noble Sherwood as the featured speaker. School had been delayed due to flooding of the Ohio River. High water was a constant worry in Maysville. The great flood of 1937 remained in the minds of local residents, and the possibility of a floodwall was often discussed.

At the service, "Pomp and Circumstance" by Elgar was performed by the high school orchestra, which I conducted. Franck's "Psalm 150" was sung by the high school chorus and the senior high girls chorus was heard in "I Will Lift My Eyes unto the Hills" by Harker.

The Maysville newspapers, the Daily Independent and the Public Ledger, were generous in reporting school activities in front page articles. In the spring of 1943 a headline read:

Maysville High School Wins State and Regional Honors

All of the Maysville High School music students taken to the music festival at Morehead by Miss Coralie Jones, their instructor, won the right to appear in the state finals at Lexington. Of the five different units entered, three of them rated superior, and one of them rated superior plus. The other unit rated excellent, but due to the fact that it was the highest rating in its category, it will go to the state meet, also.

Miss Jones in her first year of teaching in the local school, is to be commended for the fine showing of her students.

In the spring of 1943 I had my first experience preparing students for the Kentucky All-State Chorus held in Lexington in the University of Kentucky gymnasium. Nine of my students were chosen to participate: Jane Russell, first soprano; Charlotte Newell, second soprano; Anna Pearl Fowler, first alto; Peggy Parker, second alto; Donald Wood, first tenor; Glen Mattingly, second tenor; Joe Newell, second tenor; Tom Keith, first bass; and Charles Bramel, second bass. The conductor of the chorus was Frank Biddle, director of music in the Cincinnati Public Schools. Three hundred and twenty singers were in the chorus, representing thirty-seven schools. The All-State Orchestra of 60 members was directed by Eugene Wright of Columbus, Ohio. I remember sitting in the auditorium, listening to the rehearsals, and feeling an overwhelming sense of excitement.

All of my entries at the regional contest held in Morehead had won the right to compete in the state finals in Lexington. These events were: Girls' Trio: Jane Russell, Peggy Parker, and Charlotte Newell; Boys' Quartet: Don Wood, Glen Mattingly, Tom Keith and Charles Bramel; Bass Solo: Tom Keith; and Mixed Quartet: Jane Russell, Peggy Parker, Glen Mattingly and Tom Keith; Clarinet and Flute Duet: Don Wood and Tom Keith. What a thrill it was when all of my entries received the rating of superior! Because of transportation restrictions due to the war, large groups of glee clubs, bands, and orchestras did not participate in the festival of 1943.

At the annual promotion exercises held in the Maysville High School auditorium on June 16, 1943, the Junior High Girls' Glee Club presented two numbers: "Cloud Pictures" by Rich and "Vesper Hymn" by Stevenson. Tom Keith sang "Invictus" by Huhn and a Girls' Trio composed of Jane Russell, Peggy Parker, and Charlotte Newell sang "America, My Own."

The closing exercises for the school year were held late due to the high water that had been experienced that spring. School had been closed for two weeks, as water from the Ohio River covered Front Street and parts of Second Street. I had to hurry home to Bowling Green, for my wedding was June 23! There were parties and preparations to attend to. In addition, I had an impacted wisdom tooth that had to be removed – just before the wedding ceremony!

After a brief wedding trip to Cincinnati, Harold and I returned to Maysville to our furnished apartment on Third Street. The apartment was in the back of the upstairs of the home of Mr. and Mrs. Chris Kilgus, owners of the Kilgus Drug Store. We paid $40 a month for it, and I constantly worried about all this money "going down the drain." We needed to have our own home. After some persuasion, Harold agreed and we bought a house on Riverview Terrace, where we lived for many, many years. It was a lovely home, high on the hill. Our lot extended from Second Street to Third Street – all on a steeply sloping hill. I have fond memories of this home with the 49 steps leading up to it. We had a grand view of the Ohio River, and knew we were safe from floods. We even had friends staying with us, several years later, due to the flooding of the river, Ruth and Stephen Manning and their two children. We paid what seemed to us a very high price for our four-bedroom home, with large living room and lovely dining room: $7,000! What made our home even more wonderful were our neighbors – Dr. and Mrs. Harry Denham directly in front and Mr. And Mrs. John H. Clarke, across the street, next to the Denhams. We became very close to these wonderful people: Dr. Harry was our doctor and Johnny was our attorney.

My second school year: 1943-44

When school started again in the fall of 1943, our new band director came – John K. Farris. He stayed in Maysville until his retirement, and we had marvelous times together: musical events at school and singing in my choral groups as well as in the First Christian Church choir.

On December 19, 1943, the Mixed Chorus presented the Christmas cantata, "King of Kings" by Davis. This work was accompanied by an instrumental ensemble under the direction of John Farris and its members were Gayle Clark, Terell Elder, Mr. Farris, James Likins, Lloyd Moran, Frank Quigley, Vivian Vancamp, and Dorothy Wood.

I formed a Boys' Choir that sang "Silent Night" and "I Heard the Bells on Christmas Day." Soloists taking part were Gaylord Rogers, Tom Keith, Josephine Halfhill, Jane Russell, Peggy Parker, and Mary Milton Russell.

The members of the Mixed Chorus were: Pauline Brubaker, Lida Crockett, Dorothy Elrod, Mary F. Grimes, Josephine Halfhill, Winonah Jones, Gay Lambert, Bonnie Lee, Joyce Love, Martha Likins, Dorothy Marshall, Betty Morgan, Nancy Poor, Mary Julia Samuel, Martha Jane Tully, Doris Turner, Jane Wood, Betty Anderson, Marie

Cantrill, Freida Collins, Laura M. Grierson, Jane Russell, Mary M. Russell, Bonnie Cavlish, Jeanne Caproni, Joyce Davis, Anna P. Fowler, Norma Ginn, Jewell Groce, Enola Kurtz, Sarah Newell, Peggy Parker, Betty Stevenson, Margaret Strode, Anne von Thurn, Johnny Crockett, Gaylord Rogers, Ted Zweigart, Tommy Weaver, George Fitzgerald, Tommy Keith, Ronald LeForge, Frank Long, Billy Purdon, Calvin Sullivan, and Woodson Wood.

The members of the Boys' Choir were Donald Berry, Billie Joe Candy, Jimmy Clarke, Joe Conley, Joe Doyle, Billy Follmer, Kenneth Follmer, John Gantley, Bobby Harrison, Daniel Henson, Melvin Henson, Melvin Hirschfeld, Billy Ray Insko, Ray Louis Jones, Robert Likins, Bill Perrine, Nicky Pitakis, Frankie Porter, Winn Thomas, Allen Turner, and Tommy Weaver. Accompanists for the concert were Miss Lucy Woodruff and Mrs. C. S. Manning.

Thirteen students were chosen from Maysville High School to sing in the All-State Chorus to be held in Lexington in the spring of 1944: Peggy Parker, Jane Russell, Tom Keith, Oren Simmerman, Tommy Weaver, Gaylord Rogers, John Crockett, George Fitzgerald, Anna Pearl Fowler, Mary Milton Russell, Leslie Parry, Dorothy Elrod, and Josephine Halfhill. The numbers were "The Ash Grove," a Welsh folk song; "The Pedlar" by Dicks; "Verdant Meadows" by Handel; "Ifca's Castle", a Czechoslovakian folk song; "Ode to America", by Cain; "Jesus, Jesus, Rest Your Head" by John Jacob Niles; "Invitation to Harvest Meet" by Wihtol; "Laudamus Te" by Muller; and "Jesu, Word of God Incarnate" by Mozart.

Winners of the superior rating or the highest rating at the regional contest at Morehead on April 1 competed in the State Festival on Friday and Saturday. Students and their selections were: Girls' Trio: Jane Russell, Mary Milton Russell, and Peggy Parker singing "Oh, Dear, What Can the Matter Be"; Mixed Quartet: Jane Russell, Peggy Parker, Orin Simmerman, and Tom Keith singing "Madame Jeannette." Soprano solo by Jane Russell: "Ah, Love, But a Day"; Baritone Solo by Tom Keith: "The Trumpeter." Mrs. C. S. Manning was the accompanist for the solos.

All entries earned a superior rating.

One of the most exciting experiences at the state music contests happened in Memorial Hall at the University of Kentucky the next year. I had an ensemble of eight singing an eight-part number, "Orpheus With His Lute." Since the number was a cappella, I sat in the audience next to Miss Mildred Lewis, the head of the U.K. music department. The judge was in the balcony of the hall and after the group performed, he came down from the balcony and asked to see the director of the group. Thinking I had violated some rule, I quivered in my seat. Miss Lewis punched me and said, "He wants to see you." I managed to move into the aisle where he was standing and he said he wanted to shake the hand of the teacher that had taught these students. He marveled that they were not college students by the way they sang. The audience applauded. I remember distinctly that I was wearing a red suit, and my face became the color of it. That same day, the Boys' Quartet had performed and many asked me where I had found the selection they had sung. My Maysville students had captivated the audience that day.

The 1944-45 school year

In December 1944, the Christmas concert featured a pageant directed by Edna Haney and Catherine Patterson in addition to a 70-voice choir singing music appropriate to the holiday season. The accompanist for the concert was Lucy Woodruff; the costuming was prepared by Maurine Collins, assisted by Flossie Jones; James Likins was in charge of the lighting.

The choral part of the program was as follows:

Ave Verum	Mozart
A Legend	Tchaikovsky
Lo, How a Rose E'er Blooming	Praetorius
I Wonder As I Wander	arr. Niles
Josephine Halfhill, soprano	
Lullaby on Christmas Eve	Christiansen
Dorothy Elrod, Leslie Perry, Lida Crockett, Martha Jane Tully	
The Sleigh	Kountz

The choir then processed to the balcony singing "O Come, All Ye Faithful."

The cast for the pageant was: Mary, Helen Nicholas; Joseph. James Likins; Angel of the Annunciation, Jean Perrine; Angel of the Shepherds, Mary January Strode; Flower Angels, Martha Grigson, Betty Sullivan, Dorothy Wood, Christine Hawkins, Margaret Ann Duley, Betty Kreutz, Shelley Rhodes, and Catherine Graves; Stage Angels, Margaret Manley and Jane Zeigler; Small Angel, Nancy Barkley; Kings, James Ellington, Walter Maher, and Ronald LeForge; Shepherds, James Cox, Johnny Crockett, Arch Church, Tommy Browning, Allen Turner; Train Bearers, Don Candy, Billy Ball Russell, Paul Brubaker; Reader, Frank Quigley; soloists during the pageant, Josephine Halfhill, Tom Keith, Gaylord Rogers, and Barbour Kilgus.

In the spring of 1945 the vocal music department of Maysville High School presented a concert with 72 students comprising the mixed chorus, boys' chorus, girls' glee club and the modern choir. An article published in the Public Ledger described the new choir: "Much interest has been created in modern music in the last few years. Many girls' choirs have been organized for the purpose of singing modern and semi-classical music. The new chorus at the high school will sing three numbers: "Star Dust," "Tea for Two," and "When Day is Done." The accompanist for the group is Miss Lucy Woodruff. The newspaper article went on to state: "The 13 participants in the vocal department of the state music contest are members of the choir of Maysville High School. Their consistent high ratings in contest will serve as an indication of the ability of the various choruses. Due to the limitations imposed by the war on contests, there has been no provision for glee clubs at the state contest since 1941. This concert will serve as a means for the patrons and friends of the school to see what the vocal department has been working on this school year. There will be no admission charge and the public is cordially invited to attend."

In May 1945 an article in the Public Ledger stated that "Twenty-nine Maysville High School students won the right to compete in the State Music Festival in Lexington this weekend. This number includes those eligible for participation in the All-State Chorus and those who gained top rankings in the regional music festival. They were Mary Milton Russell, Norma Jean Ginn, Leslie Parry, Josephine Halfhill, Dorothy Elrod, Jewell Groce, Lida Burgess Crockett, Adolph Barnhardt,

Tommy Keith, Billy Galloway, Kenneth Reeves, Barbour Tom Kilgus, and Ted Zweigart. Tommy Keith and Josephine Halfhill will sing solos by virtue of their previous high ratings."

Instrumentalists under the direction of John Farris included Tommy Keith, Gene White, Woodson Wood, Tommy Morgan, Gayle Clark, Lloyd Moran, Dorothy Wood, Adolph Barnhart, Betty Sullivan, Ralph Calvert, Nicky Pitakis, Gus Stergeos, Catherine Whitaker, Billy Young, David Lindsay, Roy Giehls, and Louis Browning. In the vocal department; Girls' Trio I: Josephine Halfhill, Dorothy Elrod, and Norma Ginn; Girls' Trio II: Leslie Parry, Mary Milton Russell, and Jewell Groce; Mixed Quartet: Leslie Parry, Mary Milton Russell, Billy Galloway, and Tommy Keith; Male Quartet: Billy Galloway, Barbour Kilgus, Tommy Keith, and Adolph Barnhardt; a cappella choir: Leslie Parry, Dorothy Elrod, Mary Milton Russell, Jewell Groce, Billy Galloway, Barbour Kilgus, Tommy Keith and Adolph Barnhardt.

The 1945-46 school year

In October 1945, the Maysville Mixed Chorus appeared on the convention program of the Eastern Kentucky Educational Association in Ashland. The program was as follows:

I:	Ave Verum Corpus	Mozart
	Lo, A Voice to Heaven Sounding	Bortniansky
II:	Oh, Pedlar, Tell Me	arr. Krones
	Snow Legend	Clokey
	Donkey Serenade	Friml
III:	The Ash Grove	Welsh Folk Song
	The Sleigh	Kountz
IV:	Onward, Ye Peoples	Sibelius

The Maysville Ministerial Association held Good Friday Services each year at the First Christian Church. Students from Maysville High School provided music for these programs. Students were dismissed from school if they attended the services, which were held from noon to 3 p.m. At the service in 1946 a mixed quartet composed of Lida Crockett, Mary Milton Russell, Billy Galloway, and Kenneth Rees presented "All in the April Evening" by Roberton.

In the spring, several students participated in the regional music festival at Morehead, with accompaniments played by Miss Lucy Woodruff. Students and their selections were: Mixed Quartet: "All in the April Evening" by Roberton (Mary Milton Russell, Lida Crockett, Billy Galloway and Kenneth Reeves). Girls' Trio I: "Noon" by Harris (Lida Crockett, Mary Milton Russell, Mary Alice Elrod); Girls' Trio II: "Oh, Dear, What Can the Matter Be?" (Leslie Parry, Mary Milton Russell, and Jewell Groce). A cappella Choir: "Orpheus With His Lute" (Lida Crockett, Mary Milton Russell, Mary Alice Elrod, Cynthia Fowler, Billy Galloway, Buddy Jackson, Charles Clift, and Kenneth Reeves). Soprano Solo: " A Southern Song" by Ronald (Josephine Halfhill). Girls' Chorus: "The Snow Legend" by Clokey. Mixed Chorus: "May Day Carol" by Taylor. Boys' Chorus: "A Moonlit Night" by Wennerberg. Junior High Girls' Chorus: "The Quest."

A program given for the Lions Club in its meeting at Traxel's Restaurant on May 13, 1946, included the Girls' Trio II, and the soprano solo by Josephine Halfhill. John Farris presented some of his instrumental students: Billy Hirschfeld, cornet, played "Centarus" by Vandercook, accompanied by Miss Lucy Woodruff on the piano. Other selection was "Beautiful Colorado" by De Lucia played by Gayle Clark with her mother, Mrs. Herman A. Clark, at the piano.

I resigned from the Maysville City Schools at the end of the 1945-46 school year and in February 1947 our first child, Randolph Paul, was born. I enjoyed the four years I spent in the Maysville schools but was content to be a mother. Our daughter, Constance Coralie, was born in August 1949. Through this time I remained active in the music of the church, developed the Maysville Civic Chorus, and was president of the Maysville Civic Concert Series that brought many outstanding artists to the city.

CHAPTER 4: THE FIRST CHRISTIAN CHURCH
"Glory, Laud and Honor"

In the summer of 1942 I received a call from the Rev. Hilton A. Windley, minister of the Maysville First Christian Church. He offered me the position of choir director, starting in the fall when I moved to Maysville to teach in the Maysville City Schools. The church salary was $5 a week and would remain so for many years.

The choir area was in the southwest corner of the sanctuary, placed at an angle in front of the pipe organ. This very old organ had been a project of the Ladies Aid Society, a strong and active group in the church. They had insisted that a pipe organ be purchased. A reed organ had been purchased in 1883. Two or three of the older members of the congregation were opposed to using it in the church service on the grounds that its use was not scriptural. Therefore the reed organ was only used in the Sunday school services, but after a few years it was placed in the sanctuary. As early as 1907, the Ladies Aid Society proposed the purchase of a pipe organ and a great effort was made to raise the money. It was finally installed in 1909, and the public was invited to a recital to hear the "grand new pipe instrument played upon by Mr. Frederick Rogers," (Taken from *A History of the Christian Church*, Maysville, Kentucky by Gayle Braden and Coralie J. Runyon). A piano was purchased in 1929 for use in the sanctuary.

Choir directors preceding me had been Dr. G. Smoot, Boyd Muse, Miss Dolly Ford, L. B. Britten, H. Brandenberg, Addison Everett, Nicholas Brilla, and Louis Friedman. An improvement to the choir loft was made in 1896 when an elevated platform was erected there. Armchairs were used for the choir seats.

When I took over duties as choir director, the choir had approximately 12 members. Many were quite elderly and resented any changes to the way things had been done in the past. One of the oldest members resented my asking him to sit with the men's section, instead of the sopranos. He informed me that he had been sitting there for many, many years, and no one as young as I was going to move him.

I solved the problem by having the women move to the opposite side. My dear, old gentleman seemed to be placated, and made sure that he took his choir robe home every Sunday, so that no one else would accidentally use it.

I loved that choir, and as the years unfolded it grew in musical depth as I matured in musicianship. I resigned after 25 years, but came back later to work with them. Many of the singers who joined the choir in the years that I was with them are still there, presenting beautiful music each Sunday morning. We became a real family, and I am indebted to the First Christian Church for asking me to be their choir director more than 60 years ago.

I increased the membership of the choir, ever being on the alert for musicians in our community who had no church home. Many came into our church through the music program. One of the new members was a young optometrist beginning his practice with an office on Market Street. He was an excellent musician and had a fine tenor voice. It was Harold Runyon.

Harold was very active in the church, serving as deacon, elder, and chairman of the board. The church was our life, and when our children came along, they were anxious to be old enough to sing in the choir. Our son Randy served as organist during his high school years and even later, commuted from Oxford, Ohio, where he taught at Miami University, to serve again as organist for a few years. Our daughter Connie took over the duties of choir director for a short time.

On April 25, 1943, the choir of 29 singers presented an Easter cantata, "Life Eternal" by Fred Holton. Mrs. Clarence Moore was now the organist, replacing Thelma Sunier. Frances was an excellent organist and remained at that position for many years. We enjoyed our association together.

I included several of my outstanding high school students in the cantata as well as my sister, Martha Jones, a beautifully trained soprano. The high school students were Jane Russell, Peggy Parker, Glen Mattingly and Tom Keith. These young singers always answered my call to participate in our musical activities. Our minister, Hilton A. Windley, had a beautiful tenor voice and sang in the choir for this Easter cantata as well. Mrs. James Likins, a member of the choir, had a lovely soprano voice and was a faithful choir member and soloist for many years.

Soloists in the cantata were Lucy Woodruff, Tom Keith, Jane Russell, Peggy Parker, Hilton A. Windley, Martha Jones, Glen Mattingly, and Mrs. James Likins. Members of the chorus were Sopranos: Mrs. James Likins, Catherine Patterson, Laura Farrow, Mrs. Elizabeth Farrow, Mrs. Ida Goodman, Mrs. Elizabeth Robertson, Mrs. Tom Cook, Mrs. John Kluka, Jane Russell, Martha Jones, Betty Marie Anderson, Lida Burgess Crockett, Martha Myers, and Frieda Collins. Altos: Lucy Woodruff, Thelma Sunier, Ann Waits, Mrs. Conrad Rasp, Peggy Parker, and Charlotte Newell. Tenors: Glen Mattingly, Donald Wood, Harold E. Runyon, Hilton A. Windley. Basses: Addison Everett, Joseph Newell, James Likins, Jr., Charles Branble, and Thomas A. Keith.

The choir, together with several guest singers, presented "The Crucifixion" by John Stainer at a vesper service on Easter afternoon in 1945. The two soloists were Maurice Parkinson, tenor, and Tom Keith, baritone. Mr. Parkinson, a native of Covington, Tennessee, came to Maysville in the fall of 1943 as a member of the language department of Maysville High School. When he was a junior in college, he began formal voice training with Lucille Russell in Ada, Ohio. While teaching at Rives, Tennessee, he studied with a private teacher in Union City, walking five miles after school for a lesson, and returning at night; in addition he studied with Sidney Dalton, at the Nashville Conservatory of Music and with Miller Haas, Louisville, Kentucky.

The talented singers in the community who joined the choir at First Christian Church included: Gladys Parrish, Catherine Patterson, Lida Crockett, Mary Duke Gray, Pauline Todd, Josephine Halfhill, Jane Russell, Leslie Parry, Doris Loyd, Thelma Sunier, Mary Milton Russell, Elizabeth Roberson, Lucy Woodruff, Mrs. Gordon Campbell, Mrs. James Likins, Mrs. Holmes McChord, Mrs. Eugene Paynter, Barbour Kilgus, Eugene Royse, Billy Galloway, Adolph Barnhardt, Emory Rogers, Joseph Newell, James A. Likins, Jr., Kenneth Reeves, and Harold E. Runyon. Mrs. Clarence L. Moore was the organist.

On March 19, 1948, the choir again present Stainer's "The Crucifixion." The soloists for this performance were Harry Nolte, tenor, and Thomas A. Keith, baritone. The chorus was composed of Sopranos: Mrs. Brooks Mattingly, Lida Crockett, Mary Duke Gray, Josephine Halfhill, Mrs. James A. Likins, Mrs. Gordon Campbell, Mrs. E. H. Hutchison, Beulah Breeze, Mrs. Thelma Alford, and Ann Loyd. Altos: Peggy Parker, Lucy Woodruff, and Doris Loyd. Tenors: Eugene Royse, Harold E. Runyon, Harry Nolte, E. H. Hutchison, and William Jackson. Basses: Thomas Keith, Buddy Schumaker, Kenneth Ransbottom, John K. Farris, Brooks Mattingly, and Harry Hetrick.

On April 30, 1945, Arthur Wayne Braden, who was doing graduate work toward a doctorate at the University of Chicago, occupied the pulpit at First Christian. Wayne and his wife, Gayle, a native of Florida, were our guests at our apartment on East Third Street. Harold had known them at Transylvania University, and he was anxious for Wayne to become our new minister. We were thrilled when the official board called him to be our minister. He resigned in 1945 to serve as a naval chaplain in World War II, but accepted a second call to the church in 1946. In 1948 he resigned to accept a call to the Huntington Park Christian Church in California. During these two terms as minister here, Harold and I were very close to the Bradens and enjoyed their friendship in the time we had together.

During his second pastorate in Maysville, the Bradens lived with us in our house on Riverview Terrace until the parsonage was available. Gayle and I decided to research the history of the church. All we had

Randy and Connie with Harold, above, and with me, right.

was a scrap of paper that listed the 28 charter members. These people had seceded from the Baptist Church in Maysville and had formed their own church, meeting in a carpenter's shop in Graves Alley, and then later in nearby Washington, Kentucky.

Such a lack of information intrigued us, and we decided to delve into the history of our church. We spent countless hours reading newspapers of 1828 and the next several years that we found in the library. Miss Lillie Rae Pecor, the librarian, was most helpful to us. Our investigation took us to the Filson Club in Louisville, to the headquarters of the Disciples of Christ in Indianapolis, Indiana, and to the University of Chicago. We consulted court house records as well as the minutes of the Baptist Association in Kentucky. It was an adventure to seek the actual facts of the church's origin in Maysville.

We set upon the task of putting all this information in a book which the official board had printed at the Transylvania Printing Company in Lexington. The Bradens left for a pastorate in California, and I had to complete the proof-reading and write the index on my own.

A banquet to launch the book was held in the church's gymnasium-fellowship hall on November 28, 1948, with Dr. A. W. Fortune, former minister of Central Christian Church in Lexington, as the featured speaker. I was sorry that Gayle could not be there enjoy the fruits of our labor. The book received favorable comments from many sources, and I am proud that we accomplished our task of fact-finding when we only had a small scrap of information to start with.

The following editorial appeared in the Maysville Daily Independent:

In the preface of the newly published book *A History of the Christian Church of Maysville* will be found these words spoken by the Rev. John Benton Briney on the occasion of the dedication of the present church building in 1877: "Human history is constantly repeating itself; and about the best way to look into the future is by looking into the past. The philosophy of history is one of the most useful and interesting branches of study that can engage the powers of the human intellect. It is thereby that the wise observer of the facts of history is enabled to avoid the breakers upon which the barks of his predecessors have gone to pieces upon the seas of human enterprise. It is this that gives to every generation great advantage over all that have gone before it." It was with such a spirit that Mrs. Gayle Braden, wife of the former pastor, the Rev. Arthur Wayne Braden, and Mrs. Coralie J. Runyon, wife of Dr. Harold Runyon, dedicated themselves to the task of assembling data of the Christian Church since its founding in 1828. They found that the church in its 120 years has exerted an immeasurable influence upon the community and its more than 4,000 members. They realized that a past of such significance must not be forgotten.

The result has been a comprehensive, well-written and readable history of the church which is to be given to the membership at an anniversary dinner Sunday night held primarily for this purpose.

Citizens of Maysville will recognize the book as a noteworthy accomplishment. Every member of the congregation will treasure the written document which sets forth broad, historical outlines of the church and its ministers through five generations....

The Mason County Ministerial Association sponsored annual Reformation Day Services. For the second one in 1950, I was asked to provide music for this elaborate and meaningful program. They invited all the churches in Mason County to send representatives to sing in a combined choir under my direction. The following churches sent singers for a month of rehearsals held at First Christian: Sardis Christian, Mayslick Baptist, Mayslick Christian, Aberdeen Baptist, Dover Baptist, Mr. Olivet Methodist, Central Baptist, Seddon Methodist, Lawrence Creek Christian, Church of the Nativity, Washington Methodist, Minerva Methodist, Dover Christian, Mill Creek Christian, Germantown Methodist, Washington Presbyterian, Plumville Christian, Trinity Methodist, Central Methodist, First Baptist, First Presbyterian, and First Christian. The Willis Music Company of Cincinnati provided a Hammond organ without charge, and Mrs. Clarence L. Moore provided organ music for the service and accompanied the choir. The Maysville High School Concert Band, under the direction of John K. Farris, also provided stirring music for the service. The anthem "Built on a Rock" by Uggen was sung by the combined choir with Mrs. A.

F. Gilvin, soprano and John K. Farris, flute. The message, "The Glory and Challenge of the Reformation," was delivered by Dr. William A. Mueller, of Louisville, Kentucky.

The Third Annual Reformation Day Service was held on October 28, 1951, in the Maysville High School gymnasium with 1,300 in attendance. Mr. Robert Fischer, of Louisville, was heard in "The Twenty-Third Psalm" by Albert Hay Malotte, and a combined choir of 200 voices presented two anthems: "The Lord's Prayer" by Malotte and "The Battle Hymn of the Republic." The Maysville High School Concert Band, under the direction of John K. Farris, and Mrs. Clarence L. Moore at the organ, again provided music for the service. Dr. Homer W. Carpenter, Louisville, Kentucky delivered the message: "Protestantism Faces the Contemporary Crisis."

Highlighting the fourth annual observance in 1952 were two choirs numbering over 300 singers. A Youth Choir also was organized to sing for this occasion, with young people between the ages of 9-14 from nearly all the churches of the city and county comprised this group. The Youth Choir joined the Adult Choir in the anthem "The Holy City" by Adam. The Adult Choir of 200 voices sang "God of our Fathers" by Warren. Mrs. Clarence L. Moore was the organist, and pianists were Mrs. Julian Atkinson and Mrs. Lloyd McDonald, both of

The Children's Choir, about 1953.

chapter four

Flemingsburg. The Maysville High School Band under the direction of John K. Farris was heard in the prelude and postlude. I was assisted in the preparation of the music by Mrs. Philip Day, Miss Mary Denney, Mrs. Louis Cablish, and Miss Lyle Hutchison.

The Adult Choir members were: Gail Batchelor, Luisa Chenault, Nancy Austin, Norma Wells, Jackie Thomas, Evelyn Kalb, Jessie Landreth, Mildred Bane, Joyce Kirkland, Janice Jennings, Charlotte Ingram, Sue Harrison, Elizabeth Humlong, Willa Haughaboo, Betty Harding, Sophjia Hunter, Willa Landreth, Armilda Lowe, Dorothy Jean Laycock, Phillis Montanaro, Patsy Morgan, Betty Morgan, Sue Mains, Lynda McGowan, Nancy Barkley, Barbara Barnett, Polly Barbour, Gayle Applegate, Alene Allison, Thelma Arthur, Carol Osborne, Joyce Ann Thaman, Verna Ellis, Pauline Wallingford, Allene Tuel, Linda Power, Virginia Lewis, Phoebe Johnson, Patsy Howe, Janice Batchelor, Shirley Barber, Imogene Galagher, Marguerite Greenlee, Harriett Halfhill, Edwina Carmichael, Genrose Swango, Estelle Osborne, Marjorie Owens, Jean Osborne, Edith Phillips, Joyce Parker, Ann Marie Snapp, Carolyn Scott, Wilena Valentine, Hazel White, Winnie White, Nancy Wilson, Eleanor Wood, Carol Weller, Barbara Wells, Verla Mae Thomas, Ruth Soister, Betty Mae Cracraft, Carlisle Chenault, Shirley Catron, Mary Denney, Mary Frances Duane, Ruby Hawkins, Virginia Hill; Claude Huntsman, John McElroy Cochran, Wilbur Hill, Floyd Faul, Charles Finney, Maurice L. Dillon, Philip Day, Evelyn Carpenter, C. W. Christine, W. B. Collins, Louis Cablish, William Bean, W. M. Savage, Orville Rains, William Shugars, William Poynter, William Walker, Gordon Campbell, Richard Eskridge, Elmer Bussell, Wall Bacon, Leroy Hardy, Eugene McDowell, Homer L. Moore, Lewis Kilgus, Betty L. Jolly, Katherine Paynter, George W. Taylor, Evelyn Wheeler, Donald Thurber, Walter Austin, Alex Fassolitis, Lowell Ashcraft, C. E. Bailey, T. T. McDonald, James A. Moak, Ethel Morgan, Leonard Mains, Ernest Lyons, Emily Jolly, L. C. Halfhill, Kenneth Fern, Max Brand, Robert Hellard, Houston Wood, W. B. Smoot; Bob Bradford, James L. Hamm, Emery Vice, Kenneth Fern, Marion Wilson, Ted C. Gilbert, James Day, Bob Stiles, Dale Wilson, Lloyd H. White, Houston L. Wood, Wally Shelton, Bob Wilcox, Donald Combs, John Clarke, Jr., Bobby Blankenship, R. M. Baldwin, Eugene Woodward, Thomas

Brighten Your Corner

Weaver, Jack Lowe, Omar Moran, Ray Boone, Jimmy Bocock, Zebedee Brittain, George Banford, Joe F. Morgan, Clinton Hicks, William Jackson, Emory G. Rogers, Wayne Bell, K. E. Hill, A. Winn, Richard Eskridge, Dr. William Savage, and Harold E. Runyon.

The Youth Choir was composed of: Donna Root, Ruth Lyons, Gabrella Parker, Barbara Power, John Kohler, Barbara Pollitt, Carole Parker, Billy Rex Parker, Pamela Glass, Johnny Mains, Nettie Lou Cablish, Terri Lee Racel, Jerry Allen Ormes, Nelma Jean Fraley, Martha Hawkins, Jimmy Ladenburger, Donna Racel, Buddy Hall, Jerry Ray Landreth, Elveda Fraley, Carla Sue Lefler, Alice Evenburger, Jay Hardymon, Bud Baldwin, Betty Anderson, Betsy McKinivan, Dora Fannin, Tony Bellas, Benny McDowell, Maurice Dillon, Nelda Wells, Loval Weaver, Carolyn Applegate, Anne Gordon Scott, Sandra Case, Charlotte Wells, Violet Wheeler, Sammy Cablish, Jane Wood, Estil Tucker, Stan Cullen, John Collins, Robert Lane Biddle, Marceline Wheeler, Maceline Wheeler, Jimmy Bellas, Pat Barbour, Dawn Bristow, Nedra Keepers, Dana Frame, Carolyn Riddle, Mary Helen Poe, Janet McDowell, Johnny Glass, Linda Lou Glascock, Amy Kay Goodwin, Betty Mae Henson, Nora Lou Helvey, Barbara Hetrick, Kenneth Hinton, Gregory Karembellas, Shirley Mae Calvert, Juanita Thacker, Nancy Siria, Diane Scott, Jackie Yarber, Nancy Miller, Alice Montjoy,

OUR YOUTH CHOIR OF MORE THAN 100 VOICES

Patty Brown, Jo Ann Rouse, Helen Mingee, Mariln Murrell, Sue Davis, Libby Yarber, Alice Austin, Rebecca Laycock, Linda Russell, Marion Arnold, Judy Evans, Paul Bailey, Jimmy Brothers, Leneir Walker, Noel Weller, Danny Clevenger, Peggy Downing, Ruth Ann Daniels, Billy Sauer, Tarasa Travis, Lois Vanlandingham, Horace Sweet, Elizabeth Thurber, Sandra Laker, Betty Lou Sauer, Martin Sauer , Jo Allen Rawlings, Charles Bellas, Avalon Rigg, Cecil Brammer, Sally Ann Miller, Joan Boyd, Janice Blevins, Wayne Tolle, Kay Savage, Philip Hutchison, Rodney Springer, Jessie Stevenson, Mary Ann Denham, William Hardy, Ona Hardy, Jerry W. Hall, Sammy Vice, Alice Galbraith, Glenn Roberson, Barbara Hamlin, Mona Fowler, Levi Borisch, Mickey Brock, P. Montanaro, Billy Traxel, Ruby Griffith, Glenda Moran, Mary Elaine Day, Glenn Brothers, Steve Barnett, Robert Hutchison, Gene Wright, Phyllis Jefferson, Sandra Newell, John Carter, Edith Jane Daniels, Patricia Forman, Joyce Finch, Jane Goodwin, Suzanne Forman, Joan Gillespie, Bobby Humlong, Nancy Hardy, Charles Hornbeck, Bertha McDowell, Ann Morton Moore, Diana Moore, Wendell McCord, Ida Lou Eldridge, James Davis, Mollie Fox.

    Robert Fisher of Louisville was the guest soloist, and was heard in Malotte's "The Twenty-third Psalm" during the offertory.

    In the First Christian Church bulletin of March 14, 1954, the following notice appeared:

    Our Youth Choir of more than 100 voices will sing during the morning worship hour on Palm Sunday, April 11. This is always one of the high points of our church year. Rehearsals are scheduled as follows: March 17, 14, 31 (immediately after school) and on April 7 at 7 p.m. Mrs. Harold E. Runyon will direct the choir. Mrs. Clarence L. Moore will be the accompanist. Miss Lyle Hutchison is assisting in the arrangements. Mrs. William H. Sewell and Mrs. Houston Curtis are serving as choir mothers. The first rehearsal is this coming Wednesday afternoon. This choir consists of all our church school students from the first grade through the Junior High department.

    The Youth Choir joined the Chancel Choir in the presentation of "The Palms" by Fauré on Palm Sunday, April 11 and on May 2, 1954 the two choirs presented "The Holy City" by Adams.

A notice in the church bulletin of May 9, 1954 stated appreciation for the Youth Choir: "All of us were deeply thrilled last Sunday and on Palm Sunday when our Youth Choir of more than one hundred voices joined with the Adult Choir in singing to the glory of God. The direction and organization of a choir of this size is a tremendous job. We sincerely appreciate the work done by the following people: Miss Lyle Hutchison, Mrs. William Sewell, Mrs. Houston Curtis, Mrs. Ray Boone, Mrs. Clarence L. Moore, and Mrs. Harold E. Runyon."

A notice in the church bulletin of May 16, 1954 stated: "Our choir has been signally honored by receiving an invitation to play a prominent part in the forthcoming convention of Christian Churches to be held at Paris on June 25, 26, 27, and 28. Our choir will lead the worship service on Sunday evening, which is to be held at Southside Gymnasium in Paris. The choir will sing a choral introit, lead the congregation in singing the hymn "Forward Through the Ages," sing a choral call to prayer and response, sing two anthems – "Jesus, Our Lord, We Adore thee" by James and "Holy, Holy, Holy" by Spicker – and sing the choral benediction. This is a great honor which is richly deserved."

While the church was undergoing renovation in the sanctuary, services were held in the Russell Theater. Services were held there beginning on May 16, 1954 and lasted until September of that year.

On December 22, 1957, we presented Handel's "Messiah," and the soloists were Martha Jay, my sister, soprano; Phyllis Jenness, contralto and voice professor at the University of Kentucky; Aimo Kivienimi, tenor, professor at the university, and Robert Fischer, bass-baritone, who taught at Bellarmine College, in Louisville. Frances Moore was at the organ and Helen Greim was at the piano. Members of the chorus were: Mrs. E. H. Hutchison, Loretta Boone, Mrs. Winn Turner, Janice Hamilton, Mrs. Martha Poynter, Mrs. Eugene Grigson, Mrs. Claude Cummins, Mrs. Helen Ellis, Mrs. Marion Grannis, Mrs. Josephine Toncray, Mrs. Charles Finney, Mrs. Eugene Bramel, Mrs. William Yazell, Mrs. John McIntyre, Ruth Soister, Allene Tuel, Ann Lutes, Zoe Chamness, Juanita Hughes, Nancy Wilson, Sue Ellen Grannis, Dreama Thompson, Mrs. Loyd Peters, Carol Grigsby, Bonnie Lashbrooke, Jeannette Fulton, Mrs. Glynn Burke, Mary Ladenburger, Verna Ellis,

Mary Denney, Nellie Hardy, Janice Baxter, Kathy Curtis, Mrs. Robert Anderson, Mrs. Harry Denham, Mrs. Robert Hellard, Mrs. Floyd Faul, Mrs. Gibson Clark, Libby Yarber, Charlotte Shockley, Evolyn Mains, Marcele German, Barbara Lemon, Jeannine Fulton, Charlotte Ingram, Joyce Thaman, Martha Van Landingham, Harold E. Runyon, William Jackson, Eugene Bramel, John McIntyre, Robert Blankenship, Robert Likins, Ted Helbling, John Scott, Allen Woodward, George Osborne, Claude Cummins, Ray Boone, Robert L. Jones, William Yazell, James Bocock, James McDaniel, Bill Traxel, Lewis Kilgus, Steve Frasure, Robert Neu, Jack Stroud, Gayle Bess, Ronald LeForge, Randy Dailey, Wendell McCord, Terry Blatter.

On Palm Sunday, March 30, 1958, I used two choirs in the anthem. The large Children's Choir processed to the balcony, wearing their robes, and joined the Chancel Choir in singing "All Glory, Laud, and Honor" by Gillette. The members of the Children's Chorus were: Jill Arrasmith, Earylene Arrasmith, Caroline Boone, Helen Bramel, Bonnie Jean Boone, Dottie Bean, Sandra Berry, Susan Brady, Betty Bramel, Linn Brock, Diane Catron, Joy Ann Cox, Frances Crawford, Holton Cartmell, Karen Denton, D'Ann Frodge, Jimmy Finch, Mary Nell Faulkner, Glenda Finch, Anne Huntsman, Glenda Hardymon, Tommy Heidelberg, Tyra Hellard, Susan Jefferson, Allen Jackson, Donna Jackson, Tommy Jefferson, Jerry Jefferson, Jamie LeForge, Janice Lyon, Molly Lambert, Sharon Moore, Shirley Mefford, Tommy Morris, Virginia Nestor, Rita Osborne, Randy Runyon, Joyce Russell, Jan Roberts, Matha Rees, Johnnie Rawlings, Connie Runyon, Anne Steffen, Philip Sagraves, Kathy Sanders, Ann Thompson, Sharon Tolle, Billie Jo Toncray, and Regina Vice.

In 1957 I became a den mother as my son Randy was a Cub Scout and ten years of age. I knew very little about knot tying and the various other things required of den mothers. We met at the church, and I did my very best to serve my little troop. Jean Somerville came to my aid as a co-den mother.

In the summer of 1957 I was a counselor at Camp Alleghany in West Virginia. I took Connie with me to Junior Camp and Randy went to nearby Camp Greenbrier, a boys' camp. I went to West Virginia a week early to learn how to row the boat. The only way to get to Camp

Alleghany was to park your car in the parking lot, go down to the river, and row over to the other side. It took a lot of training and a lot of patience, for the boat kept going around in circles! I finally made it to the other side and qualified as a counselor. We had a wonderful time. I had four girls in my tent. They were from various places in the east. One, I recall, was from Washington, D.C., the daughter of a politician. They were sweet girls, though somewhat spoiled. The tent had a wooden floor and we rolled up the side flaps during the day. The tents were arranged in a rectangle around a quadrangle. I was asked by the owner of the camp, Nancy Worthington, if I would play the bugle – "Taps" at night and "Reveille" at morning. I contacted John Farris and he instructed me over the telephone on how to play the bugle. I worked at it and managed somehow to utter some toots. In spite of that, I was soon replaced by a more experienced bugler.

In the first week when we were being trained to be counselors, we were taught how to make up a cot. It had to be tight as a drum, and we had to flip a nickel on top of the covers to make sure it was taut. The whole summer was fun. My job was to teach choral music and I had a colleague who taught at St. Bartholomew Boys School in New York City. She was not used to the outdoor life. We tripped to the wash-house where we took a shower and brushed our teeth, and she wore a Malibu-trimmed robe and satin slippers.

At night we gathered in the large recreation hall and had skits and various fun things with the campers. I helped the drama teacher, who was from Lynchburg College, as well as rode the truck that came once a week to pick up the laundry from each tent. Miss Worthington lived in a comfortable house on the hill, and she invited me up to play bridge with two other lucky counselors. On some clear nights we took our girls up on the hill where Uncle Billy, an authority on the skies, would explain and point out the constellations. We also learned archery from him – a fun and difficult sport.

The teachers presided at the dining tables in the mess-hall. We would serve the food and see that proper manners were observed. This was great training for the girls, and one that should not be neglected.

We counselors kept one good outfit in the dry room for our rare trips into the outside world. After saving up our leisure hours, four of us would go over to the Greenbrier Resort Hotel or the Homestead for lunch. We had a great time being together, but we always had to row that boat even late at night as we tip-toed back to our tent and sleeping girls.

It was a good summer and it was great to have my children near at hand. Harold came up a few times, and I would get permission from Miss Worthington to be with him and spend the night at the General Lewis Inn in nearby Lewisburg. We also visited Randy at the Greenbrier Camp.

When I was gone from the church that summer, Dr. Claude E. Cummins, Jr. directed the Chancel Choir and Bill Traxel directed the Youth Choir in the absence of Robert Jones, our youth minister, who was on vacation.

I was honored for 25 years' service to the church.

Chapter 5: The Civic Chorus
"Singing With a Star"

Early in January 1951, I felt that an adult chorus including the outstanding voices of the community should be formed. The Maysville Civic Chorus was organized with 50 selected members. Its purpose was to present to Maysville and the surrounding communities music of outstanding and cultural worth and to enhance the art of choral singing. I was the conductor of the group and Mrs. Julian Atkinson, choral director of Flemingsburg High School, was the accompanist. The membership in the chorus included many educators in Maysville and Mason County schools. Both the superintendent of the county schools, Emory G. Rogers, and the superintendent of the city schools, Ted C. Gilbert, were members of the group, as well as John K. Farris, and Mrs. Floyd Faul and Miss Mary Denney, voice instructors in the Maysville schools. Other teachers who joined were Mrs. Emory H. Hutchison of Maysville High School, Miss Mildred Bane of Washington School, Mrs. Katherine Paynter of Maysville Forest Avenue School, Mr. Emory Hutchison and Mrs. A. L. Gilvin of Aberdeen, Ohio High School. The officers of the group were Dr. W. M. Savage, president; Ted C. Gilbert, vice-president; Katherine Paynter, secretary-treasurer; Mary Denney and Verna Ellis, librarians. The Board of Directors was composed of Dr. W. H. Cartmell, Mrs. Robert A. Cochran III, Robert N. Adair, Harold Cunning, Mrs. L. L. Browning, Mrs. Bertrand Walz, Rev. James A. Moak, and James A. Finch, Jr.

The chorus gave many concerts both in Maysville and out of town. Some of the out-of-town concerts were at the Eastern Kentucky Educators' Meeting held in Ashland; Brooksville Methodist Church, Presbyterian Church, West Union, Ohio; and the Presbyterian Church, Manchester, Ohio. Maysville concerts included the presentation of "The Seven Last Words of Christ" by Theodore Dubois on April 9, 1952. The Daily Independent printed this review of the concert:
Silence Eloquent Tribute to "The Seven Last Words"
Rarely are the walls that divide men broken down.

But that is how it was for a Maysville audience last night as its members shared the beauty of Dubois' "The Seven Last Words of Christ."

For a brief hour, there was in every heart a sense of communication between him and His Maker. For a brief hour, there was a bond between chorister and heaven, between neighbor and neighbor.

A Holy Week audience will be forever grateful to the newly formed Civic Choral Group and to its director, Mrs. Harold E. Runyon, for a presentation that in its majesty and solemn grandeur proved a noble prelude to the Good Friday commemoration of the Crucifixion of Our Lord and the birth of Christianity with His Resurrection on Easter morning.

Maysville is grateful, too, to the guest soloists for superb renditions of the cantata. These soloists were Miss Mary Frances Duane, soprano, Mr. Robert Fischer, baritone, of Louisville, and Mr. Steely Veach, of Cincinnati.

And an equal measure of appreciation must go to Mr. Paul Ramseier, of Louisville, and to Mrs. C. Stephen Manning, Maysville's very fine organist.

But the triumph of the evening was the choir itself, a choir beautifully trained and lifting their voices in prayerful acknowledgement of the debt due their Redeemer.

Perhaps the greatest tribute that Maysville could pay the Civic Choral Group was the tribute of silence. Almost without a word the congregation assembled in the Maysville school auditorium left the hall—all carrying in their hearts the meaningful words they had just heard.

The concert was subsequently rebroadcast on our local radio station, WFTM.

In December the local paper reported:
Civic Chorus to Sing on Public Square
Providing a Christmas atmosphere for Maysville shoppers next Tuesday evening will be the music presented around the Market Street Christmas tree by members of the Civic Chorus under the direction of Mrs. Harold E. Runyon. The chorus will present an hour's program of

Christmas music under the auspices of the Maysville Younger Woman's Club.

As the shoppers go from store to store making their last minute purchases they will indeed feel "there's a song in the air," as the choral group renders songs that are both old and new and ever popular.

A special feature of the evening will be several Christmas carols presented by Homer G. Cablish, Jr., on the marimba.

In charge of the event is a committee composed of Mrs. Lewis Kilgus, Mrs. Robert Anderson, and Mrs. Oscar Brock.

Immediately following the concert the chorus will go caroling around many of the Maysville homes and thereafter will gather at the home of Dr. and Mrs. Harold E. Runyon on Riverview Terrace for a Christmas party.

Here refreshments will be served to the members and their husbands or wives. Guests will also be members of the board of directors of the chorus.

In 1953 the Civic Chorus was pleased to be asked to sing at the ceremonies attending the world premiere of "The Stars Are Singing," starring Maysville native Rosemary Clooney. The choir was positioned in a semi-circle outside the Russell Theater and presented several selections. Rosemary, a beautiful, very small blonde girl, was escorted into the theater where she sang some of the numbers she had made so popular. After the showing of the film, Harold and I were guests of our mayor, Rebecca Hord, for a dinner party honoring the participants on this gala evening. Rosemary sang again to a warm and enthusiastic audience. Earlier in the day a parade was held in downtown Maysville with Rosemary riding in a convertible wearing a full-length mink coat. The members of Beta Sigma Phi entertained her with a reception where she graciously accepted becoming our "sister" in this sorority. I was privileged as an officer of the group to take part in the ceremony.

In April 1954, the Civic Chorus presented a concert of sacred music in the Brooksville Methodist Church. Soloists with the choir were Mrs. Alex Fassolitis in Franck's "O, Lord, Most Holy," Dale Wilson in "The Holy City," Wayne Bell in "The Battle Hymn of the Republic," and Miss Genrose Swango in Dickinson's "Christmas Lullabye of the

Fourteenth Century." Mrs. Julian Atkinson, piano, and Mrs. Clarence L. Moore, organ, provided the accompaniments, and the Rev. James A. Moak was the narrator.

Dr. W. M. Savage, president of the chorus, received a very complimentary letter from Henry Moreland, Superintendent, Brooksville Methodist Church School: "It is difficult for me to put into words the amount of appreciation that is due to your chorus for the wonderful music that was presented by your group last Sunday. I thank you graciously. Many words of appreciation were spoken that evening, but the next day I heard compliments galore from nearly everyone present."

The Daily Independent on May 19, 1954 reported:
Civic Chorus Is Accorded Ovation, Concert Termed Wonderful Success

Maysville's very fine Civic Chorus sang its way once more into the hearts of a town audience last night as it scored its top success in its ninth concert – and the first for which anyone ever paid to hear these choristers sing.

"They sang like professionals" was a typical comment of the audience, which was well pleased with two facts: the musicianship and showmanship of the choristers. The chorus, of course, boasts the best voices and musicians in town, in the county, and even so far as Ripley.

Even Mrs. Harold E. Runyon, the choir's director, confided she would have been proud for Fred Waring, whose school she attended a summer ago, to have seen the presentation of such numbers as "Jalouise" because of its showmanship and of such numbers as "Holy, Holy, Holy" because this festival number is rarely sung by big choruses and represents a major undertaking.

As handled by the Maysville chorus of 50 voices it was very well done. Mrs. Charles Finney, of Ripley, was the soloist.

The concert had a happy beginning in "A Hymn to Music," which is the choral setting of Chopin's well-loved Etude in E and has a beautiful piano score therein for Miss Janice Head to handle. In this presentation the soloist was Maysville's well-loved Miss Genrose Swango.

In the "Jalousie" number two high school teenagers who learned ballroom dancing under Mrs. Arnold E. Brown gracefully danced the tango through three choruses with maracas, gourds, and claves as an accompaniment to two pianos and percussion.

These same South American rhythm instruments were used again in three numbers from the play "South Pacific" sung by an all male chorus which used gestures for a very picturesque number with color and swing. Outstanding here was the rendition of "In My Arms."

The women's chorus won acclaim with the singing of "While We're Young" as well as "Spin, Spin, My Darling Daughter." In this number Jane Wood and Sandra Case were on the stage before a spinning wheel, with each attired in pioneer costume and sunbonnet as the mother tried to persuade the daughter to spin.

A soul-stirring rendition that kept the audience breathless was the singing of "The Battle Hymn of the Republic" in which Mr. John Buel was the soloist. Again there were two pianos, percussion and tympani for accompaniment.

The concert closed on a patriotic note that brought goose bumps and spine tingling to the fore. This was the singing of "Give Me Your Tired, Your Poor," an Irving Berlin song for which the Statue of Liberty towered above the chorus. For this number Virginia Carnes, high school

Our Beta Sigma Phi ceremony with Rosemary Clooney (fifth from left). I am first from left.

senior at Minerva who was chosen from among candidates selected by every high school, presented a quality appearance draped in white and with a gold crown atop her head as she held aloft the torch of liberty.

Miss Janice Head was the pianist for most of the numbers and she was heard in two compositions, "Reflections on the Water" by Debussy and "Spanish Dance" by de Falla. Miss Head, teacher at Orangeburg, is a brilliant musician. Also serving as accompanist when two pianos were used was Mrs. Floyd Faul, music instructor in the city schools and a member of the chorus.

Mr. Gene Manley was the percussionist and Mrs. Clarence L. Wood, sponsor of the sponsoring Beta Sigma Phi Sorority, presented the chorus. Sorority members served as ushers.

Party is Given for Civic Chorus

Sponsoring last night's concert was the Beta Sigma Phi Sorority, which after all expenses are paid will turn over the proceeds of the concert to the chorus for operating expenses. The chorus obtains no public financial support and its members sing "for the fun of it."

After the concert the sorority entertained the chorus, their husbands and dates with a supper at the home of Mrs. Richard Thaman in East Second Street.

Here follows a list of members of the Civic Chorus throughout the years: Mrs. Robert Anderson, Mollie Andrews, Betty Atherton, Mrs. Charles Bailey, Mildred Bane, Polly Barbour, Mrs. William Chamness, Mrs. Florence Christine, Mrs. Woodrow Crum, Mrs. Harry Denham, Mary Denny, Mrs. N. J. Denton, Verna Ellis, Mrs. Eugene Ensor, Mrs. Richard Eskridge, Mrs. Alex Fassolitis, Mrs. Charles Finney, Mrs. George Fotos, Mrs. Floyd Fasul, Mrs. A. F. Gilvin, Mrs. Marion Grannis, Mrs. Robert Hellard, Mrs. E. H. Hutchison, Charlotte Ingram, Mrs. Lewis Kilgus, Mrs. John W. Kirk, Mrs. Allen Kohler, Mrs. James A. Moak, Mrs. Homer Moore, Mrs. William McChord, Carol Osborne, Mrs. George Osborne, Joyce Parker, Mrs. William Poynter, Katherine Paynter, Mrs. Jay Simpson, Mrs. W. M. Savage, Betty Schwartz, Betty Schmitz, Mrs. William Shugars, Katherine Stewart, Mary Strode, Genrose Swango, Mrs. Eddie Taylor, Allene Tuel, Wilena Valentine, Mrs. Robert Williams, Caryl Wilson, Mrs. Clarence Wood, Mrs.

Donald Wood, Mrs. Donald Wood, Jr., Mrs Houston Wood, Wayne Bell, Donald Belval, James Bocock, Ray Boone, John Buel, Houston Curtis, William De Ruyter, Richard Eskridge, John K. Farris, George Fotos, Ted Gilbert, Darrell Hill, Emory Hill, E. H. Hutchison, William Insko, William Jackson, Sam King, Allen Kohler, James Marshall, Brooks Mattingly, Loyd Moran, George R. Osborne, Jack Perrine, Joe Phillips, Emory G. Rogers, Harold E. Runyon, W. M. Savage, Dale Wilson, Donald Wood, Donald Wood, Jr., Houston Wood.

Chapter 6: The Ripley Years
"The Little Choir That Could"

In 1954 I accepted the position of director of music in the Ripley Schools in Ripley, Ohio. My good friend Marjorie Finney, a member of the Civic Chorus, had urged me to teach in Ripley, where she was the organist of the Presbyterian Church. I had not taught in the public schools for eight years while I was raising my children though I had been busy teaching private lessons, directing the Civic Chorus, and conducting the music program at the First Christian Church. The thought of teaching in a high school again appealed to me, and I accepted the job. Ripley was only seven miles down the river from Maysville, and my daughter Connie could attend kindergarten there.

On the first day at the high school I was met by a young man, Denny Keller, who shook hands with me and welcomed me to his school. From that day on down the years, Denny and I have become great friends, and I treasure his friendship as well as my friendship with his wife, Carolanne, and their two children, Dennison and Caroline.

I found out quickly that the chorus had been singing from a mimeographed sheet of words, rather than reading choral music. I remedied that situation and developed a mixed chorus and a boys' chorus that read music from the printed score. In the spring I took the newly founded boys' chorus to a contest held in Wilmington, Ohio. The number of singers required for a chorus was 16, and since we had 17 in our group, I had decided to enter. I chose a five-part selection, "Sunset" by Schubert. We received a rating of superior, went on to the state finals and received another superior, to my great joy. This was an auspicious beginning for my years at Ripley. The accompanist was Marcele Germann, a very talented young lady in the school.

I found a vacant room and had the old upright piano rolled down the hall from the cafeteria, where we had chorus rehearsals, to my "voice studio." Some of my outstanding voice students were Janet Shirden, Loretta Boone, Eileen Davis, Tony Helbling, Teddy Helbling, Benny Scott, and Roger Neu.

The next year I took three choruses to the regional music festival.

Each one claimed the number one rating of superior, and then went on to Columbus where they again received superiors. The Boys' Chorus now had 25 members, the Girls' Chorus had 30, and the Mixed Chorus totaled 55 singers. Ripley was the only school in Brown County to receive the top rating. Aberdeen, which sent a Girls' Chorus for the first time, with Nick Marinaro directing, received a rating of excellent. All five Ripley soloists received the superior rating, went on to the state finals and received that rating again. The Boys' Octet and Girls' Ensemble each received superior. The Mixed Ensemble of eight voices received the rating of excellent.

The years at Ripley proved to be a great experience. When I asked my principal-superintendent, Mr. Charles Phillips, if we could buy risers for the choruses, he replied that there was no money for this. I assured him not to worry, because I thought of the risers the Civic Chorus had purchased that were being stored at First Christian. I had stopped the rehearsals of that group since I was teaching in Ripley, so we inherited the risers, and I brought them to Ripley. There was also a good deal of music stored in a filing cabinet at the Maysville church that I also was able to use with my Ripley singers. I asked Mr. Phillips if we could purchase choir robes, and he answered that my ideals were too high for Ripley. I assured him not to worry – I would get them. I went to the J. C. Penny store in Maysville, purchased several bolts of material, and took them to the Home Economics teacher at the school. The students were measured – the choir had grown to nearly 80 members by now – and robes were made: black skirts and white surplices. This was the outfit for several years, and the choir looked wonderful in their homemade robes. Later we were able to purchase robes and stoles from a choir-outfitting company.

The first year I taught in the elementary school in Ripley, the kindergarten presented a playlette called "The Circus." My daughter Connie was in this group. I enjoyed teaching the music for this program. In 1980 an article in the Ripley Bee described the program we gave in 1955:

When members of the kindergarten class "graduated," there were two students whose parents "graduated" 25 years ago. Robert Faulkner Sidwell and John Phillips were members of the class who received diplomas on May 24, 1955. This week, their children, Heather Sidwell and Justin Phillips, were a part of the 1980 class. The 1955 class presented a circus performance and pupils were Hermie Scott as Ringmaster, Connie Runyon, Donna Griffith, Pam Wilson, Roger Gifford, Roger Kinnett, Junior Polley, Paul Haas, Roddy Milligan, John Phillips, Wendall Lam, Portia Rossman, Donna Poff, Charlene Thompson, Roger Stidham, Larry Kratzer, Greg Pfeffer, Diana Edminsten, Steve Wilson, Donna Rice, Linda Carpenter, Roberta Faulkner, Dennis Herrell, Kathy Gooding, Roberta Jackson, Judy Dwelly, Jeannine Johnson, Beverly List, Jo Ann Grubenhoff, and Dorothy Rankin. Mrs. Anna Lemon was the teacher of this big circus performance.

I also taught the 7th and 8th grades at the parochial school, St. Michael's. The nuns were helpful and appreciative of my efforts. When I would go to the contest, they said they would remember me in their prayers. Surely this had a great effect on the outcome.

On Dec. 15, 1958, the Ripley High School choir was featured in a Christmas program with the Lexington Orchestra, under the direction of Eric Kahlson. In announcing the selection of the Ripley choir, the Lexington Herald recalled the choir's achievements. In the state finals of music competition all three choruses of the school – the Mixed Chorus, the Boys' Chorus and the Girls' Chorus – had received unanimous ratings

Teaching in Ripley High School, around 1956.

of superior. I was a member of the first violin section of the Lexington Orchestra, and was overjoyed that my choir had been chosen to sing. I included a number written by Kentucky's famous composer, John Jacob Niles, and he was very complimentary to me after the concert on their rendition of it. Mr. Kahlson, the conductor, came to the Ripley school to work with the students before the concert, and he was delightfully surprised at the high quality of their singing.

The high school work became more involved. Since the soloists, choruses, and ensembles received superiors in the contests, I had the audacity to enter a competition for an appearance on the national program of the Music Educators' Convention in Chicago. I was thrilled when I received word that my chorus had been selected as one of the finalists. In a letter from Charles H. Benner, who was the president of the Ohio Music Educators Association, with offices at Ohio State University, he wrote on November 15, 1958:

> Dear Mrs. Runyon:
>
> It is a pleasure to inform you that the Ripley High School Chorus has been selected as on of the eight groups to be nominated to the North Central Committee in charge of the Chicago Convention Program. If selected to appear in Chicago, we shall be most happy to have the Ripley group represent the quality of work being done by music educators in Ohio.

As I was a member of the Lexington Orchestra, and I went to Lexington on Monday nights for a long rehearsal. On arriving home one night, my husband said I had a telephone call to return no matter what time it was. Dr. Benner, who had sent the letter, asked if I was standing or sitting. He suggested I sit down and told me that the committee had decided that one chorus would represent Ohio, and that it was the Ripley High School Choir. He then said to me, "Now, young lady, you have your work cut out for you." I was sure that he felt I had better live up to the committee's expectations. The other contestants that had been nominated in the first round of competition were Miami University's Men's Glee Club, the Ohio State University Chorus, and a chorus from

Massilon, Ohio. My chorus from tiny Ripley had won over these very fine groups!

The next day I told Mr. Phillips the good news, and he said to me: "How are we going to pay for this trip?" Looking out the window and seeing a large elm, I responded, "Mr. Phillips, don't you know that money does grow on trees?" We then proceeded to raise the money for the trip. We made money in various ways and it came easily. I asked all the students who lived on a farm that raised tobacco to donate a hand of tobacco to the choir. They started bringing in the hands. We kept them in a room at school, and finally the janitor said, "I wish you would get this tobacco out of here. It is certainly overflowing." It was sent to the tobacco warehouse in Ripley and made a huge pile. I went to the auction sale, and they asked me to stand on top of the tobacco mound. They helped me to the top, and I made a little talk about what we were doing. The buyers were very generous and we received a good deal of money from this unusual sale.

We had 95 in the chorus and it required three buses. We traveled by Trailways. We not only enjoyed the trip up and back, but we planned a sight-seeing adventure for the students in Chicago and for the 14 chaperones that accompanied our group. When we were introduced by Dr. Benner in the ballroom of the Conrad Hilton Hotel before we sang, he told the story about how we raised the money. "This little tiny

The Ripley High School Chorus, around 1959.

town on the Ohio River was a real Cinderella story. This little town had a fine, big chorus, and to raise money the students brought in a hand of tobacco each." We stayed at the Conrad Hilton, took our own risers, and I stood in the lobby before mealtimes and doled out a dollar to each student for food. There was a steakhouse not far from the hotel that advertised a steak for $1.50. I told them to save on breakfast and lunch and they could enjoy a fine supper!

Mr. Phillips and I thought it would be a good education for our boys and girls to have a fine dinner in the hotel's dining room. I began to teach them the protocol, the "Emily Post" of dining, and brought a place setting of china and silver, a napkin, and a goblet to the school. I placed it on the piano and taught all of my students which fork and knife to use. After planning the menu with the head of the dining room at the hotel, we prepared the students for dining in a very elegant way. I told the girls that if they wore a black dress, high heeled-shoes, white gloves, and a string of pearls, they could go anywhere. I told the boys to wear a jacket, tie, and long-sleeved white shirt. These were the outfits the students wore as we entered the Persian Dining Room at the Conrad Hilton. As we entered there was only one table occupied, and the rest were reserved for us. At that table sat a man and a woman. Later I found out that it was Dr. Benner and the supervisor of music for the State of Ohio. They told me later that they had remarked to each other, "What group is this coming in the hotel? It must be a girls' finishing school with them all dressed alike. Oh, there are boys. It must be a choir." They came over and spoke to me, and found out that it was the little Cinderella Choir from Ripley. They were very complimentary of how we looked, but they had yet to hear us sing.

The next day was the day of the performance. I held a rehearsal in the baggage storage room in the hotel on the floor that also housed the offices of the hotel. I got the students crammed into the room and stood on a trunk and warmed them up. I worked on one of the numbers by Brahms, which was sung in German, titled "Da Unten im Tale." When I was working on this I noticed something very beautiful happened on one measure. Whenever this happens, I call attention to it – this is the SOUND. I stopped and repeated that part, and we did it again and again. I told them that this was the sound that I wanted. An amazing thing happened at this point. Someone looked in at the door. Then more people came to the door, and then the hall was filled with the clerical workers from the offices. They were listening to us, and the 95 students were in a sort of trance as we went down to the ballroom. At the end of the concert there was a standing ovation that wouldn't quit. There were several nuns in the audience, and they remarked to me that they had felt a very moving experience when the heard the Rachmaninoff "Ave Maria." The choir filed out amid all the applause. We filed into the exhibit hall, and all along the way people would say, "Oh, you are the choir that is taking Chicago by storm." After viewing the exhibits we took a trip around Chicago on Lake Michigan by boat. Upon arriving back at the hotel, I was told that the Chicago Sun had tried many times to contact me. They had heard about the choir's reception and a reporter wanted the story. I returned his call and was interviewed over the phone. He wanted to know about the school and about its size and how a school of this size could have a choir with almost all the students in it. He wanted to know how I had developed a choir of such caliber to be chosen to represent the state of Ohio at a national conference. The article appeared in the Chicago Sun the next day. I still want to read that reporter's story.

When the choir was preparing for the Chicago trip the school was closed because of high water. The Ohio River invaded Main Street

The chorus, about 1959.

and the school was shut off from the main part of town. I decided that this would be a fine time to practice and told the students they had to get there by boat, no matter what. The City of Ripley furnished a boat called "The Duck." It was a large boat, and the students rode it over the high water to dry land and could then walk to the school. I could drive from Maysville to the school, which was on the east side of town. The students made it safely to the practice, and I had them all day. We were now ready for our Chicago trip.

In the spring of 1959 as we were getting ready for Chicago, I had an unexpected operation. While I was in the hospital in Maysville I was worried about the success of the money-raising activities. To my surprise Mr. Phillips, who had always been so skeptical about raising money, came to see me in the hospital, opened a sack and poured money all over the bed. "This is what we raised while you were ill." Everyone had pitched in to help. The whole town felt that they had a part in this. An interesting by-note is that when we would return from contests as far away as Columbus, Mansfield, or up near the Great Lakes, we would be met at the edge of Ripley by a fire engine and a police escort bringing the three buses in! The bus drivers would stop along the way, and telephone the Ripley police department to say that we would arrive at 1 or 2 a.m.. Many times we would drive up to the home of Mr. Phillips at these early hours to show him the awards we had received. At the toot of the horn, he would come out in robe and slippers, and we would present him with the fruits of our labors. Oh, these were wonderful times in Ripley. I do not know of any other situation where a chorus has been met year after year with an escort of policemen and fire engines on returning from a music contest. These are memories I shall never forget.

Fred Anderson, an artist who had worked for the Walt Disney Studios in California, lived in Ripley and owned a small restaurant next to the Pepsi Cola Bottling Company. He and I became friends and he designed "sets" for my concerts. One of the most memorable was the time he converted the stage into the interior of a church. In the back were stained glass windows, copied after Chartres Cathedral. In front was a railing for the high school choir. I had a boys' choir of elementary students from the school in Ripley at the foot of the stage. It was a beautiful concert and one like the ones the Presbyterian minister said he would like to "bottle it and open it years later."

Arch Verville of Maysville was a man of many hobbies. At the time I was teaching in Ripley, his hobby was making recordings. He bought the latest equipment and kept abreast of the latest techniques. He recorded my chorus many times and made a record of many of their numbers. The music department of Miami University later had these numbers on the recording bound into a booklet that was used for choral conducting classes.

The High School Choir was invited to sing on the Ruth Lyons Show in Cincinnati, a popular show somewhat like the Today Show. News, weather, and interesting topics were on the agenda daily. Many people visited the show and made up the audience. We were thrilled to be asked. On the show Ruth Lyons interviewed me and the choir sang several numbers. She and Peter Grant, the newscaster on the program, joined the choir on the last number.

The Cincinnati Times Start sent a reporter to interview me when we were preparing for the trip to Chicago. He asked me how I was able to build such an outstanding choir in such a small school. I replied, "Because we had no chairs." He used this headline for a full-page story. Since the choir rehearsed in the cafeteria immediately after lunch, there was no time to gather up chairs, nor was there enough space for the 95 who were in the chorus. I devised a routine of seeing how fast a team of boys, headed by Roger Neu, could set up the risers and wheel the piano into place. I held a watch, and they were eager to see if they could beat their own records. We only had three minutes to get the lunchroom cleared, swept, and the risers made ready. I heartily recommend this for all choral conductors. When the students entered and went to their assigned places, music was distributed on the first and third rows and the rehearsal could begin without delay. The correct singing posture was much easier to achieve when the students were already standing.

I had always prided myself on an ability to make everyone sing. I nearly met my match at Ripley. One day I heard several boys talking around the water fountain outside the choral room. One had a very melodious, deep voice, and I wanted to know who he was. I rushed out into the hall, found the young man, and invited him to join the choir. He was astounded, and said that he could not sing at all. I told him I could see to that. We worked and worked. I used all the tricks I knew for him to find his singing voice, but he only managed one note accurately. That was fine – it was a good sound – on the E flat below middle C. I told him to be ready with that one, lovely sound whenever I pointed to him. He would be like a cymbal player in a symphony orchestra. One must wait and wait until the moment arrived for his part in the music. He joined the choir, was delighted to be a part of it, and sang his one note in the Chicago performance with a great sense of accomplishment. I called him "my boy with the absolute pitch."

My elementary music classes met in the auditorium of the Ripley Elementary School. The floor was uneven, due to the many times flood-waters had covered it. The piano was an ancient upright, and I was constantly moving it around. On one fateful morning my team of fourth-grade movers moved a little too rapidly, and the piano crashed over on its back. I shall never forget the dreadful sight of the piano, flat on the floor, and its keys yawning up at me. I dismissed the class, told the school principal that I had to leave, went straight to Mr. Phillips' office. I told him what I had done, and that I was resigning. He told me to cheer up. He was delighted, for now he could purchase the new piano that he had been wishing for. Needless to say, I am cautious about moving any pianos. I have to turn my back when any are moved.

Chapter 7:
The Mason County Years: The 1960s
"Building a Legacy"

The superintendent of the Mason County Schools, Mr. Hubert Hume, kept calling me for several years while I was teaching in Ripley to ask if I was ready "to come home" and teach in the Mason County Schools. I always said no, and he would hang up abruptly. When he made his call in the spring of 1960 he told me that I must come home and teach in the new Central High School. The idea appealed to me and I accepted his offer.

The new high school replaced Mayslick, Minerva and Orangeburg High Schools. Grades one through eight remained in the following schools: Washington, Lewisburg, Sardis, Dover, Rectorville, Mayslick, Minerva, and Orangeburg. Two elementary schools for black children were in the county system: Minerva and Mayslick. My job was to teach in all these schools. In a sense I was returning to where I had begun – Orangeburg.

In May 1960 the Daily Independent reported:

> Mrs. Harold E. Runyon, an outstanding musical director, yesterday was elected supervisor of music in the Mason County Schools and instructor of vocal music in the new Mason County High School…
>
> Mrs. Runyon's six-year tenure of service at Ripley was marked by rare excellence, her pupils repeatedly having taken district and state honors. She was head of the vocal music department of the Maysville High School 1942-1946.
>
> The former Coralie Jones of Bowling Green, Mrs. Runyon first taught at Orangeburg and then was with the Maysville system for four years…
>
> In 1958 Mrs. Runyon was named a member of the Ohio state committee for the selection of music to be used in state competition. Mrs. Runyon, who has also attended clinics at Bucknell, Pennsylvania, and at the University of Delaware at Newark, is director of the choir at the First Christian Church

and past director of the Civic Chorus. For a number of years she has directed the Festival of Faith Chorus.

Mrs. Runyon is the mother of two children, Randy, 13 and Connie, 11.

When I discovered that I had 75 girls and three boys enrolled in the Mason County High School choral program, I asked the principal, Mr. Elza Whalen, if I could interest more boys in the chorus. He told me I had to wait until the next year, but I said that I needed them now. I suggested that since we were a new school, many new statistics were in order and I would like to see every boy in the high school and make a record of his height, color of hair and color of eyes. Mr. Whalen was intrigued with this unusual plan, pushed the piano into the classrooms, and I began my search for talent! When each boy came down to the piano, I sounded a bass note (E-flat, usually) and urged him to mumble a sound. If it sounded promising, I would whisper to him, "I am forming a boys' glee club and can only take 40 students. Do you want to be in it?" I soon reached my quota and enlarged the music department considerably! Mr. Whalen was a wonderful sport with this hare-brained scheme, and I am indebted to him for helping me to make a good start.

I soon found that there was an enormous amount of talent in the students now enrolled in music. I formed a girls' chorus, a mixed chorus, a boys' glee club and small ensembles, and worked with solo voices. My music room was in a trailer while the large gymnasium was being built. This building had wonderful acoustics for small programs, and I enjoyed being in it for the first few years.

I also wanted to train the classroom teachers to be eager to teach music in the individual schools, and I presented an idea to Mr. Hume, our superintendent. He liked the idea and contacted Morehead State University to ask them to provide college instructors to come to Mason County and do a workshop in elementary music and give college credit for it! It worked, and all the teachers in the eight schools attended and enjoyed the experience, especially the college credit. The head of the music department, Dr. Duncan, conducted the workshop. One evening he brought a new faculty member, Mr. James Ross Beane, voice and choral instructor at Morehead, to present ideas the attendees could use with changing voices. Meeting Mr. Beane was an important milestone in my career in Mason County. He and I became good friends and I learned much from him about choral conducting and voice production. His wife, Anne, later taught at Morehead as well, and she and I became close friends. On first meeting of Jim Beane, he asked if I would play in the orchestra for a touring production of "Amahl and the Night Visitors" being produced by the New York cast. I enjoyed being a part of the group and learned much from the professional people involved. I later became a member of the Morehead University String Quartet and we had some wonderful sessions together. In the ensuing years, I was asked many times if I would teach at the university in Morehead. I was urged to start a string program at Breckinridge Training School in Morehead and to teach string classes at the college. Each time I declined, because I had much to do in the Mason County Schools, and I was just getting started.

I asked Mr. Whalen if we could purchase choir robes for my 70-voice choir. He said it was all right with him, but I had to raise the money. We set upon a moneymaking project. The Clover Leaf Dairy would buy back the black handles used to connect two bottles of milk. Radio station WFTM gave me all its old 78 records, and we sold them in an empty store on Market Street. We sold a truckload of records, many of which would be of great value today. We operated a New-to-You second-hand store that we set up in the upstairs of a building that Harold and I had purchased in 1960 for his office. We soon had the

The new fieldhouse, around 1960. My choir room was in the lower level.

money to buy blue choir robes with white and gold reversible stoles. I had two large boxes made in which to keep them, and the boxes went with us on the buses when we went to music contests. It was a rather strange way of handling robes – doling them out rather than letting the students take them home. I don't know why I thought this was best.

From the very beginning in the fall of 1960, the choral program, with its unusual method of recruiting boys, was outstanding. The students were proud of it, and this is essential for success. Our first concert was held on December 19, 1960, at the Washington School gymnasium. The 75-voice Concert Choir presented "The Song of Christmas" by Roy Ringwald, with Arthur Henderson, a junior at the high school, as narrator. My 130-voice Girls' Chorus sang "The Snow" by Elgar. Soloists taking part were Sue Fraysure, Sharon Lunsford, Mary Elaine Day, Carrie Stears, Billy Gilbert, and David Harney. Accompanists were Charlotte Griffith and Anna Mac Cox, piano, and Mrs. Clarence L. Moore, organ. The George Fotos Piano and Organ Company of Maysville furnished the piano and organ, and the lighting effects were under the direction of Mr. Carlton Fields, an outstanding African American science teacher at the high school.

In the spring of 1961 the Mason County Concert Choir and Girls' Chorus entered the music contest at Morehead and each received the rating of superior.

The Mason County High School Girls' Chorus, around 1965.

On the second annual Christmas Concert, held December 20, 1961, the accompanists were Charlotte Grifffith and Caryl Jane Worthington, an 8th grade student. Caryl Jane became an outstanding accompanist for the high school choruses and was selected to be the accompanist for the All-State Chorus in Louisville in 1967 and also in Bowling Green in 1968. She won the Kentucky Association of Women's Clubs State Piano contest in 1965. While attending the University of Kentucky she was the accompanist for the University Chorus and the Kentucky Opera Association in Lexington, and she was the accompanist for Mrs. Naomi Armstrong of the university faculty. After graduation, she became a professional accompanist in Chicago. One of my happiest memories is how I began training Caryl Jane to accompany the choral groups. I gave her the music in the summer that would be used in the forthcoming year. I held sessions in our music trailer and insisted that she keep one eye on me and the other on the music. She always did.

A glance at the program for this concert reveals that great choral literature was becoming the hallmark of the choirs and choruses of the Mason County Schools. Featured on the program were two major works: The Bach cantata "For Us A Child Is Born" and the "Song of Christmas" by Roy Ringwald. Soloists in the latter were Mary Elaine Day, Fay Rawlings, Howard Curtis, Marsha Wheat, and Donald Rosser. Arthur Henderson was the narrator for this work. The Boys' Glee Club that I had promised when I surveyed all the boys in the new Mason County High School was in full swing, and they presented a group of Christmas carols.

At the spring concert on May 11, 1962, more than 200 students performed in the Washington School Auditorium, where we were still

The Mason County High School Chorus, around 1969.

holding our concerts. Featured on the concert were the Concert Choir, the Ninth Grade Girls' Chorus, The Boys' Glee Club, the Senior Girls' Chorus, the Madrigal Singers, a girls' trio and four girls' ensembles. The accompanists were Charlotte Griffith and Caryl Jane Worthington.

At the Christmas Concert in 1962 two major works were presented: Britten's "Ceremony of Carols" by the Girls' Chorus and Buxtehude's "Rejoice, Beloved Christians" by the Concert Choir. Accompanying the choral groups were Caryl Jane Worthington, piano, and Randy Runyon, organ.

On the 1963 Christmas concert two major works were presented, the "Ceremony of Carols" by Benjamin Britten and the Dietrich Buxtehude cantata "Rejoice, Beloved Christians."

The groups had become quite large in the early 1960's: Girls' Chorus: 115 voices; the Freshmen Girls' Chorus: 55 voices; the Boys' Glee Club: 80 voices.

The Daily Independent printed the following article on April 26, 1964:

Concert Given Ovation

The robed concert choir from Mason County High School gave a superb performance last night as Mrs. Harold E. Runyon presented her vocal students in annual concert at the Washington School. The chorus presented "The Last Words of David" by Thompson and with such effectiveness that the capacity audience found the moment memorable. The crescendos here and the ability of the pupils in voice control were noteworthy. The choir came back for the closing number – this time the girls in formals and the boys in dinner jackets – to sing selections from "The Music Man." It was a triumphant, happy ending. The Boys' Ensemble was outstanding, as if they were full adults. One critic named the basses as "fabulous." The Madrigal Singers, again in formal attire, gave a series of numbers to show ability to sing in quick tempo and changing numbers without a bobble. They sang a cappella without a director.

Probably the best thing the boys did was "The Battle of Jericho." It was in four voice parts and it was terrific. In the Girls' Chorus it was beautiful to behold as well as to hear "The

Snow" with Mary Manning at the harp, Randy Runyon, flute, and Connie Runyon, alto flute.

On April 18, 1967, the Daily Independent reported:
Vocal Concert Provides Talent

The Mason County High School Vocal Music Department's concert last night in the fieldhouse under the direction of Mrs. Harold E. Runyon represented the culmination of many long hours of work on a highly ambitious program with very fine results.

Mrs. Runyon's students gave their best for a large audience that thoroughly enjoyed renditions by the Concert Choir, the Girls' Chorus, the Madrigal Singers, and the Boy's Glee Club.

Special mention should be made of the outstanding soprano solo work of Miss Billy Faye Brierley in Schubert's "Mass in G," and the rendition of Giannini's "Tell Me, O Blue, Blue Sky." Her ambition is to be a concert singer, and this shouldn't be too hard to accomplish.

The range of music performed by the various groups touched on the old and the new. Handel and Bach were used from the old school while Hindemith's "Three Chansons" came from the contemporary field. Also heard were Broadway selections by Lerner and Lowe and Rodgers and Hammerstein.

The overall vocal color of the program was splendid considering that many of the works are college material. Casals, Schubert, Bach, and several others aren't heard on the high school level unless there is an exceptional teacher.

Especially pleasing were several selections by the Girls' Chorus. They included "Psalm 42" by Rhea, and the "Agnus Dei" from Faure's "Requiem."

The Madrigals scored with several numbers, especially "The Swan" by Gibbons.

Mrs. C. Stephen Manning and Miss Debbie King were the piano accompanists.

Brighten Your Corner

Students at Washington Elementary School gave a memorable concert on December 19, 1968. Students in the entire school participated, from grades one through eight, and many later became soloists in the high school choirs. The program follows:

    We Wish You a Merry Christmas   English
    Away in a Manger   Luther
        Kim Bailey, Sarah Claybrooke, Susie Huff, soloists
    O Come Little Children   German
        Linda Turner, Soloist
    Zumba, Zumba   Brazilian
        Julie Green, Gay Hall, Judy Robinson, Jerome
        Grandison, David Browning, Instrumentalists
    Go Tell It On the Mountain   American
        Kent Marinaro, soloist
First and Second Grades
    Jesus in the Manger   Polish
        Mary Wood, Pam Hargett, Susan Hickerson, Terry Jackson, Lesley Reynolds, Allen Stitt, Mike Bramel, Randy Coburn, Keith Gragston, Kelly Calvert,

Sue Hord, Rebecca Pickrell

Semi-Chorus

    The Snow Lay on the Ground   American
    The March of the Three Kings   French
    Still, Still, Still   German

        Sam Greenbaum and Tim Marinaro, Soloists

Third and Fourth Grade Chorus

    The Birthday of a King   Neidlinger

        Jeff Danner, Martin Lowe, Jerry Wallen, Paul Stitt, Tommy Royse

Semi-Chorus

    Masters in This Hall   French
    He Is Born   French

        Bedouin Duncan, Regina Welch, Carol Fritz, Karen Tuel, Cecilia Marshall, Connie Lowe, Wendy Paul, Debra Murray, Katherine Browning, Susan Hamm, Debbie Striplin, Karen Crockett

Semi-Chorus

    What Child Is This   English

Fifth and Sixth Grade Chorus

    Praise Ye the Lord of Hosts   Saint-Saens
    'Twas the Night Before Christmas   Simeone

The Seventh and Eighth Grade Chorus

    Mrs. Ruth Manning and Mrs. Coralie Runyon, Vocal Music Instructors

    Patti Hord and Patricia Mattingly, Accompanists

The Mason County High School Concert Choir was invited to perform with the Lexington Youth Symphony Orchestra for a concert on February 9, 1969, to be held in Haggin Auditorium on the campus of Transylvania University. The choir of 88 voices performed Vivaldi's "Gloria" and Vaughan-Williams' "Serenade to Music." Soloists were Billie Brierly, soprano, Karen Ross, mezzo-soprano, Mike Franklin, bass, and Billy Henson. Joseph Ceo was the conductor of the Lexington Youth Symphony. The event was sponsored by the Kentucky Arts

Commission. The Lexington Herald reviewed the concert in its February 10 issue:

> The highly professional chorus from Mason County High School and the most competent and personable director, Mrs. Coralie Runyon, was a great addition to the program.
>
> Mrs. Runyon conducted the chorus and orchestras in Vivaldi's "Gloria." This outstanding chorus has extraordinary blend and a velvety texture. The voices are extremely mature and well rehearsed. Both orchestra and chorus had good feeling for this Baroque number.
>
> "Serenade to Music" by Ralph Vaughan-Williams was introduced by Lydia Hodson, Lexington Children's Theater, who read from the Merchant of Venice, Act 5, Scene 1, the text from which this Ralph Vaughan-Williams number was taken. The strength and lyricism of this work were manifested by both groups with great expressivity. The full chorus displayed superb blend and style, decrescendoing to the truly beautiful pianissimo. Misses Stewart and Ross were soloists with William Henson and Dan Kemplin. All four young people were capable vocalists, and turned in strong performances. Particularly impressive were the passages with harp, violas, clarinet and soloists.

This concert was repeated in Maysville on February 16 at the Mason County Fieldhouse. This article appeared in the local paper:

> **Sunday's Symphony Concert to be Rare Musical Event**
>
> When certain people say certain things, the meaning comes through "loud and clear."
>
> This is what Coralie Runyon means when she says, "The festival of the Arts Concert to be given this Sunday by the Central Kentucky Youth Symphony with the Mason County High School Concert Choir will be marvelous."
>
> Mrs. Runyon will be conducting the choral group and Joseph Ceo will be the conductor of the Youth Symphony,
>
> By now it is generally known that the performance in Lexington last Sunday was better than perfect as some of the

critics are saying.

Mrs. Runyon is expecting as much of the concert Sunday afternoon at three o'clock in the Fieldhouse.

Mrs. Runyon is especially gratified that the concert Sunday will recognize the beginning string students who will be studying music under Peter Schaffer in a program sponsored by the Maysville Community College. The students will be asked to be seated together.

Outstanding soloists during the 1960s were Marla Wheat, Mary Elaine Day, Kay Rawlings, Howard Curtis, Donald Rosser, Brenda Kirk, Billie Brierley, Debbie King, Jan Towler, Jerry Dempsey, Jerry Zeigler, Brenda Parker, Janice Day, Charlotte Griffith, Kay Rawlings, Linda Ensor, Mike Franklin, Charles Calvert, Marla Kalb, Kelly Fritz, Toni Lewis, Tim Marinaro, and Marla Wilson. I stayed after school every day and encouraged students to take part in a voice class to learn the rudiments of solo singing. Many beautiful voices were discovered by students and teacher alike. I had many excellent accompanists for the various choruses. In the 1960s these were: Kathy Wright, Patti Hord, Debbie King, Caryl Jane Worthington, and Charlotte Griffith.

A review of the programs presented by the choruses and choirs beginning in the 1960s and continuing into 1982 would show that great literature become the trademark of these groups. I was frequently called upon to conduct workshops about building a fine choral program. I was a firm believer that proper literature was a primary factor in the choir's excellence. Some of the major works sung by the choruses in concert were: Francis Poulenc, "Gloria"; Benjamin Britten, "Ceremony

The Mason County High School Chorus, around 1970.

of Carols"; Felix Mendelssohn, "Elijah"; Norman Dello Joio, "A Jubilant Song"; Paul Hindemith, "Chansons"; George Frederic Handel, "Messiah"; Gabriel Fauré, "Requiem"; Maurice Duruflé, "Requiem"; Jacobus Gallus, "Haec Dies" for double choir; Johann Sebastian Bach, "Christmas Cantata"; Roy Ringwald, "The Song of Christmas"; Antonio Vivaldi, "Magnificat"; Johannes Brahms, "A German Requiem"; Ralph Vaughan-Williams, "Serenade to Music"; Gian Carlo Menotti, "Amahl and the Night Visitors"; Karl Korte, "Songs of Innocence"; Franz-Joseph Haydn, "Mass in B-Flat"; Johann Pachelbel, "Magnificat"; Randall Thompson, "Pueri Hebraeorum" for double choir; Bach, "Come, Jesu"; Haydn, "Mass in Time of War"; Carl Orff, "Carmina Burana", Ludwig van Beethoven, the fourth movement from the Ninth Symphony.

Chapter 8: The Mason County Years: The Trip To England
"The Impossible Dream"

In the spring of 1968 the following article appeared in the local newspaper:

MCHS Concert Choir Is Invited to Music Festival in Britain

The concert choir of Mason County High School, under the direction of Coralie J. Runyon, has received an invitation to participate in the Seventh Annual American Festival in Britain.

The festival is to be held in the ancient town of Kendal in the Lake District of Northunberland, and the festival performance for the Mason County Choir is from June 26 to July 15. The choir would have a dozen performances during the three weeks' stay.

Also between performances the students would have an opportunity to visit such famous places as the Globe Theater, Stratford-on-Avon, and tour the British Isles.

Earlier Mrs. Runyon had been invited to submit a tape recording of the choir, and the invitation was the result of that recording.

Mrs. Runyon is asking all parents of students in the choir to assemble in the choral room of the high school at 8 p.m. At that time they will discuss the details of the invitation and the feasibility of accepting the invitation.

Mason County choral groups under the capable direction of Mrs. Runyon have repeatedly earned superior ratings at the regional music festivals.

On May 21, 1968 the Daily Independent reported:

Concert Choir Sees Jaunt to Europe Okay
Wheels are Set in Motion Tuesday

Mason County High School Concert Choir may well

be on its way to Britain if the enthusiasm of the 150 persons present at a meeting last night at the school is any indication. They said, "Let's go."

Mrs. Harold Runyon's elite group of choristers has received an invitation to participate in the Seventh Annual American Festival to be held in the ancient town of Kendal and the Lake District of Northern England.

The sum of $40,000 is the amount it will take to finance the trip for the approximately 75-member choir.

Members of the choir, their parents, and other interested persons met with Mrs. Runyon last night at the school to discuss the feasibility of accepting the invitation. There seemed to be no doubt that all are in favor of accepting. What is needed now is to find the money.

Ed Smith will call Governor Louie Nunn to ask for his assistance and Dr. Mitchell B. Denham said he will be working with Congressman John Watts in the State Department to see what the two representatives could do.

Ken Ransbottom was elected the chairman to head the committee in charge of working out the financial arrangements for the trip. Mrs. Billy Ross was elected secretary and Elza Whalen was named as treasurer.

Mrs. Runyon explained the details for the trip and what would be needed, such as costumes for the choir. An apparel committee also was named. This committee is composed of Mrs. Duke Clary, Mrs. Emerson Zeigler, Jr., Mrs. Merrill Vice, and Mrs. Robinson.

A publicity committee is composed of Mrs. E. A.. Smith, Mrs. Gordon Ward, Mrs. Houston Curtis, Mrs. Mildred Smith, and Mrs. Margaret Wallingford.

No date has been set and plans are being formulated for the Concert Choir to perform at Mason County in approximately two weeks. Fred Chumbler and Merrill Vice were named to head a ticket committee with 5000 tickets to be sold for $2 each in the hopes of filling the Fieldhouse.

Mr. Smith, Mr. Ransbottom, Billy Ross, and William

Calvert will be in charge of contacting merchants for donations.

A second meeting will be held Monday night, May 27, at 6 p.m. Contributions may be mailed to the Mason County Concert Choir Fund in care of Elza Whalen.

Another article in the newspaper reported that Clyde Barbour, owner of Clyde Super Value stores in Aberdeen and Maysville, announced that he would sponsor two shows, the proceeds of which would go into the choir fund. The Paul Dixon Show will come to Maysville on a Saturday night. The Notables will put on a Sunday night show, and the choir will present a concert prior to their departure.

The entire community was gracious in its support of fund raising and the trip became a reality.

Sixty-four students and 12 chaperones left the high school at 3:30 a.m. on school buses. One bus was used exclusively for the luggage. Clyde Barbour sent his car with the school bus mechanic for the drivers to return in – leaving the buses in Detroit in storage, paid for by the Restoration Arts Theatre. There was a huge crowd at the school, though it was so dark we could not see without the aid of the one flashlight in the crowd. Amid all the confusion and excitement, the students were gathered by their assigned chaperones for roll-check, passport-check, and the safe-keeping of traveller's checks. We arrived in Detroit about 1:30 p.m. and went to the home of James Allen Jones for lunch and orientation. We then boarded two American Electra propeller planes for the trip to New York. This was the first airplane ride for the majority of our students and chaperones. After landing at Kennedy we boarded buses for the Sabena Airlines terminal. We met Charlie Calvert, who had obtained a passport in Washington. After boarding the 173-passenger Sabena chartered jet, we were served a meal that included steak and wine for the adults. We arrived at Manchester and met our two tour guides, Margaret Pighills and Jennie Abbot, two charming English ladies. They became wonderful friends and did many special things for us. (One of our chaperones, Mildred Bane, returned to England the next summer to visit them.) We stayed in guest houses in Windermere. My group included seven boys: Johnny Calvert, Bob and Barry Jones,

David Grigson, Bill Wheat, Darrell Moore, and Mike Marinaro.

On Sunday, June 29, after a breakfast of grapefruit sections, cereal, Danish bacon, English muffins, eggs, toast and marmalade, coffee or tea, we attended services at a small Methodist Church nearby. We went to the Hydro Hotel for lunch and met the gracious and interesting manager, John Tovey.

We ate our meals at this hotel while in Windermere, and Mr. Tovey became fond of our group. He came to America to visit us the next year, and Maysville rolled out the red carpet to entertain him. He became a world-renowned chef, and we heard from him for many years. He said he came to Maysville because he had to hear the choir sing again! After a rehearsal at the hotel, we boarded our busses for our first concert in Wharton at the Parish Church of St. Oswald, an 11th-century church. The American flag flies here because this is the church of the forebears of George Washington. The vicar greeted us, took us to the church and afterwards to the parish house for robing. We participated in an evensong; the local choir was very good. I was pleased to see that my students knelt for the prayers. After the service the vicar explained the historical relics of the ancient church.

Our program that followed the evensong service consisted of the first three number of the Schubert "Mass in G," "I Will Praise thee, O Lord," by Nystedt, "Round About the Starry Throne," by Handel and "Honor and Glory" by Bach. I stood in the high pulpit with my music behind me! It was somewhat awkward. The acoustics of the church were thrilling, and the choir sounded huge. Mrs. Abott and Mrs. Pighills were impressed, and the students were thrilled beyond words.

On Monday we gave a concert on her majesty's ship, The Teal, on Lake Windermere. A photographer, Mr. Tweedie, was assigned to cover the story, and he was so impressed with the group that he followed all of our concerts. We sang outside, inside, and on top of the deck. The crowd was pleased and asked for more. The girls wore red, white, and blue blazers and white skirts; the boys wore navy blue blazers and navy blue pants for this boat trip. At 8:15 p.m. the choir gave a concert in the ballroom of the Hydro. We had been advertised as "the Kentucky group."

chapter eight

The next day we visited the Wordsworth Cottage and museum and other sights around the countryside. We gave another concert in the hotel ballroom that evening to a full house with many standing in the hall. I talked about the music to this enthusiastic audience. I met a couple from the United States who attended the concert. He was a professor at the University of Maryland, and he gave me a pound note for "the kids." Mrs. Abbott took Harold and me, Dorcas and Ed Smith to a real pub that evening. The bar was built on an old bed taken from an English castle. We sat in front of the fire and listened to the English songs the young men sang.

On Wednesday we went to a reception given by the mayor of Kendal. He was resplendent in a mink trimmed robe. The town clerk wore a grey wig. The choir was asked to sing and we were interviewed by a reporter. After lunch at the Hydro, we went back to Kendal to visit Abbott Hall Museum. The performance that night was in Dent in Shropshire at St. Andrew's Church. Visiting Dent is like walking through the pages of a medieval history book. The road to Dent was

England, 1968.

very narrow so the busses had to be exchanged in Kendal for shorter and narrower ones. When we met another bus on the road – after much squeezing to pass – we then had to back up to a wider spot. We also had to wait for a herd of sheep to pass – very picturesque and quaint. The driver was the soul of courtesy and patience. The church was established around the year 1180. It was a great old church serving a small, typical English village with cobblestone streets, population 500. The view of the hills and the rock walls was absolutely breath-taking. After the concert we were entertained in the school – coffee, tea, and cookies. Everyone was friendly and warm in their praise of the group. Boys from the Salisbury School were there with their masters. Some of our group struck up friendships, and one wrote to Sandi Smith later. The owner of a store opened his shop so we could buy cards showing the village and the hills.

Thursday, July 4, 1968 was such a marvelous day! Mr. Jones accompanied us and we stopped in Leeds for a luncheon he had arranged for us at the Queen's Hotel. The menu included Cornish hen, ham, and a birthday cake for me and champagne for our table of adults. We had stopped at an abbey, ruins that had been destroyed when Henry VIII had ordered all the lead to be removed in 1538. The ruins are beautiful. We arrived at Durham Cathedral at evensong. We sat in the back of the cathedral and listened to the beautiful organ and choir during the closing part of the service. Then we toured the cathedral and discovered the statue of Bishop Shute Barrington. The inscription at the base of the white marble statue reads "This Public Tribute Is Erected To the Memory of Shute Barrington Thirty five Years Bishop of Durham Who died March 25, 1826 in the 92nd Year of His Age and 57th of His Episcopate In His Works of Piety and Munificence He Being Dead Yet Speaketh" Since my mother was a Barrington and her lineage goes back to England, I was anxious to visit the cathedral and the castle where the bishops lived. The cathedral was started in the year 999. In the castle we saw a large picture of Bishop Barrington. He was famous for having discovered a door of perfect Norman architecture that had been plastered over years before. We sang in the Royal Chapel of the Castle, "I Will Praise Thee, O Lord."

chapter eight

On July 5, Mr. Tovey arranged a dinner in honor of my birthday in "Dinner at 8:30," his private dining room. I have never eaten such a marvelous meal! After dinner we attended a late show at the Century Theatre – a sort of vaudeville. I took all the students. The master of ceremonies announced my birthday! The show was not very good (in fact I fell asleep), but it was interesting to see the English sense of humor. That afternoon on our tour of the countryside we visited the home of Beatrix Potter, author of the Peter Rabbit stories, and saw the Druid's Circle.

On Saturday, July 6, we went to Kendal to attend the market on the streets that had become a ritual. We left for Barrow, stopping at the Abbey Ruins and the choir posed for pictures taken by Mr. Tweedie for an English magazine. We presented a concert for a gala at the Home of the Blind in Barrow. The residents asked for pictures of the choir so they could be hung on the wall. Later we attended a performance of "West Side Story" by a group of actors that were also participating in the American Festival in Britain.

On Sunday afternoon Mrs. Pighills took us to her 300-year home in the Long Sleddale Valley. This is untrammeled 11th-century England – the view is breathtaking. The home is surrounded by small mountains that are treeless, but have lovely stone fences. Their son, an artist studying architecture at Oxford, was there and was pleasant and interesting to talk to. The Pighills returned us to the hotel where we enjoyed a high tea and then the choir sang two anthems at the evensong service at the Kendal Parish church. This is a very beautiful church – five aisles – with excellent acoustics. After returning to Windemere we strolled down by the lake and the shopping area in Bowness, stopping at a restaurant where Eldon Jordan joined us for a late snack.

I spent Monday morning cashing traveler's checks for the students at Martins Bank. This large transaction seemed to throw the bank into a complete state of chaos. Later in the day we left for Barrow where we gave a concert at the Grammar School for Boys. The auditorium was filled – the mayor and his wife were in attendance having arrived in their Rolls Royce, their chauffeur standing by attentively. Mr. Tweedie was there and took pictures. After our concert the boys' choir from the school sang several numbers for us: "Kedron" by Roberton, "Ave

Verum" by Mozart, "Sourwood Mountain" and Handel's "And the Glory of the Lord." They were very fine and sang SATB arrangements. The music master was a charming young Scotsman.

The next day we left early for a visit to the Cartmel Priory. This is truly as beautiful as a cathedral, only on a smaller scale. The prior was very gracious and showed us about the church. He explained the priceless relics and antiquities owned by the Priory – a Vinegar Bible, an early edition of Spencer's "Faerie Queen," now kept in a vault with books written in 1450. The choir of the church is exceedingly beautiful with carvings on the posts depicting everything mentioned in the four Gospels. We hated to leave, but had to rush on to Keswick. The country was unbelievably beautiful. That night Mr. Tovey entertained Harold and me, the director of the Century Theatre, and its leading actor at "Dinner at 8:30."

On July 11 we presented our third concert in the ballroom of the Hydro Hotel. The crowd was immense – standing room only. We started each concert with "God Save the Queen" and then "The Star Spangled Banner," and ended each with "The Battle Hymn of the Republic." Mr.

Singing near the ruins of an abbey.

chapter eight

Tovey spoke to the audience after applause and applause. With tears in his eyes he said how much these young people had come to mean so much to him. "If we could send these kids to Vietnam there would be no more war – no more Nasser and Egypt and Israeli conflict." A long line of people told me how the young people had exhibited musical worth and excellence beyond expression. There were many Americans in the audience and one sought me out saying that he had heard about this choir while he was in London, and he had come to Windermere to hear them! I was flabbergasted to learn that he was Mr. Forbes, on a sabbatical from Phillip Exeter Academy where one of my very special students, Christopher Browning, was attending school. Our kids were suffused in tears at all the adulation and praise uttered from the throng of people for success strikes deep into the hearts of us all. We shall all hold dear to our hearts beautiful Windermere and the graciousness of the people we were privileged to meet.

One of the most challenging experiences of my life was the program we presented at a school for young men sent there to be toughened up. It was a large, rather beautiful building, and we assembled in the auditorium. When we began to sing there was booing and catcalls! I was amazed and wondered what I could possibly do to win their attention. After the first number, I turned to the audience and gave a small talk on the evolution of music down through the ages. I tossed the program planned aside and introduced the Madrigal Singers, who presented a few numbers. By this time the audience was somewhat interested and attentive. Then we proceeded to "Gypsy in My Soul" and ended with the music from "The Man of La Mancha." At that point these tough young men were calling for encores. There was a social hour and during the refreshments, the boys made friends with our group. Several ran to the buses and said they were going to go where we went! They taught us some songs, among which was "The Green Bottle Song." What started out as a disaster turned out to be a success. The music from these earnest young singers won over the tough, scoffing young English boys.

The next day the northern affiliate of the BBC did a documentary with the Madrigal Singers performing in the garden of the Hydro Hotel. I didn't get to see it when it was shown, but many people stopped me and asked if I was the conductor of "those American kids" they saw on the telly! After the taping, Mr. Tovey had arranged a high tea for us in a special drawing room. It was quite elegant – the English know how to do it!

On Wednesday we traveled to Edinburgh, Scotland, for a wonderful day of sightseeing, visiting the castle on the hill, and shopping.

A special dance was given at the Lakeside Hotel for our group. The girls looked gorgeous in their lovely gowns and I especially remember Miss Mildred Bane in her pale blue formal. The boys from Barrow with their wonderful Scottish music master were also guests at the dance. It was a marvelous evening in a lovely setting on the other side of the lake.

On Thursday we gave a concert at Zion Chapel Church. The mayor and his wife were in attendance. He wore a necklace with the medallion of his high office. A tea followed honoring the choir. We returned to the Hydro where we gave a concert at 9:30 p.m.in the ballroom. This was one of the high moments in my life – standing room only and an audience that begged and begged for encores. We all knew the Impossible Dream had come true.

Our final concert was at St. Michael's Church, Brough, Westmoreland, a beautiful church. The priest, the Rev. A. T. Snowden, was most gracious to us and invited me to the Parish House to meet his wife and rest before the concert. After the concert he stood, went to the altar and said the following words: "Every Sunday morning at half past eight when I raise my arms in such a manner to praise the Lord, our Heavenly Father, a flood of my experiences go through my mind. I will remember you not as a name but as a part of the heavenly force. The sound of your voices will join the angels and archangels in praising our Heavenly Father. This church is over 1,000 years old, and after your singing tonight, you will be a part of this church forever more." The students were all visibly touched, and many had tears streaming down their faces. This was our last concert in a part of the world that was so beautiful – the people so overwhelmingly gracious and kind – that emotions were at the breaking point. We were entertained with a supper in the parish hall and left Brough, where we were told that all the proceeds from the concerts made by the "young men and women

chapter eight

from across the seas" would go to the Children's Relief in Biafra, Africa. Seven thousand pounds had been raised for these starving children.

On the return trip from Brough, David Grigson, one of the members of the choir, suffered an unfortunate accident. He was asleep on the bus when it rounded a curve and he fell to the floor. The next morning we took him to the hospital in Kendal for an x-ray and examination. The doctor advised that he be hospitalized and not go on to London with the rest of the group. We left him behind reluctantly. He was not alone, however. The choir had made many friends at the Hydro and the guesthouses where they were staying. And they took turns to see that he would not be lonely. I had stayed with him all night when we took him to the clinic to see the doctor. I went to the hospital to check on him and he assured me "there is nothing to worry about." When I went to the office of the hospital to pay for his stay there I was told that there was no charge at all for their socialized medical plan took care of visitors to England. John Tovey was wonderful to David and later put him on the "bullet" train so that he could join us in London.

In London we stayed at the Regency Palace Hotel. Our buses and two guides, Mrs. Pighills and Mrs. Abbott, accompanied us for our four-day stay. On the first evening we dressed in our formal attire and had a steak dinner in the main dining room. We saw two plays: "Man of La Mancha" and "the Boyfriend." We took a side trip to the Kennedy

Singing on Lake Windemere.

Memorial at Runnymede where the Magna Carta was signed. There the choir sang "The Star Spangled Banner."

We were invited as special guests to Westminster Abbey to attend services. We were seated in the Poet's Corner, to the right of the high altar. At the time of communion we were escorted by the ushers to kneel at the rail and partake of the sacrament. It was a sacred moment to all of us. After the service we toured the Abbey, viewing Churchill's place of burial and those of the monarchs entombed there. After boarding the busses the students were absolutely silent for a long time. The solemnity of the service, the rite of communion in that awesome place, and the history all about us kept the hearts and minds of all to inward thoughts.

On Wednesday we left London for the Manchester airport. Two seats had been taken off on the chartered Sabena plane so that David could lie down. We had two nurses, Fay and Kay Rawlings, as chaperones and he was in wonderful hands. We took off at 2:25 p.m. on a beautiful day with the sun brightly shining. Our two guides and two bus drivers waved goodbye from the observation deck and the choir sang "God Save the Queen" and "The Star Spangled Banner." They called to me midst tears of sadness in leaving beautiful England, "Mrs. Runyon, we love you."

We passed over Liverpool Bay, out over the Irish Sea, and above gorgeous fleecy clouds that look like huge mounds of meringue. Between patches of clouds the patchwork of towns and farms lay beneath. We landed at Shannon Airport, Ireland, at 3:15 p.m., rushed into the airport and started madly shopping. I bought a few gifts – jam, cookies, and tea cakes. Back on the plane we were served snacks to "tide us over" before dinner: ham, roast beef, and egg sandwiches, Danish pastry, two chocolate bars, and coffee.

It is impossible to describe the beauty of pure sky over clouds that stretch in endless sheets of white. At times the ocean can be seen clearly through openings in the cloud formations – ripples that appear as a giant washboard. The blue of the ocean is terrific – a gorgeous blue, as is the sky.

Dinner was served at 7:45 p.m.: crabmeat cocktail, hard-boiled egg and tomatoes, red wine, hard roll, cheese, Bing cherries, apricots on a tray, filet mignon, celery, creamed potatoes, and buttered bread. After dinner the kids sang the entire Mass and everything they had sung in England.

After landing in Detroit, Sabena airlines put us on a chartered small plane and we landed in the airport in Aberdeen, Ohio. The radio station had asked people to line the runways with their cars with lights on. We were met by what looked like the entire town – as conquering heroes arriving home.

Members of the choir were: Rickey Alexander, Debbie Biddle, Gary Biddle, Michael Bolden, Mattie Bolden, Jean Bryant, Johnny Calvert, Carol Chumbler, Christy Clark, Joyce Clark, Libby Clay, Mary E. Cooper, Cathy Curtis, George Day, Patricia Fox, Larry Fulton, Ninnette Gifford, Debbie Ginn, David Grigson, Jane Henderson, Jo Ann Henderson, Peggy Hendricks, Mike Hesler, Donna Hinson, Patti Hord, Melanie Humphries, Diana Jackson, Barry Jones, Robert Jones, Eldon Jordan, Nancy King, Debbie Lawler, Paul Lofton, Jesse Mains, Mike Marinaro, Dale Marshall, Patty McCormick, Darell Moore, Vickie Moore, Debbie Moran, Paul Mullikin, Sharon Murphy, Bobby Myers, Diana Neff, Howard Owens, Ann Parker, Mary Ransbottom, Cherry Reed, Bill Riley, Connie Robinson, Karen Ross, Linda Russell, Connie Sapp, Sandi Smith, Shelly Tolle, Patti Vice, Lenore Wallingford, Mickey Wallingford, Mona Ward, Bill Wheat, Lyde Worthington, Kathy Wright, and Jerry Zeigler.

Chaperones were: Miss Mildred Bane, Miss Janice Tabb, Miss Ann Thompson, Kenneth Ransbottom, Thomas Bailey, Misses Fay and Kay Rawlings, Charles Calvert, Mr. And Mrs. Ed Smith, Dr. and Mrs. Harold E. Runyon.

The complete program for the American Festival in Britain:

I: Mass in G   Schubert
   Kyrie, Gloria, Credo, Sanctus et Benedictus, Agnus Dei
   Karen Ross, Soprano; Gary Biddle, Tenor;
   Paul Mullikin, Baritone
II: Praise the Lord   Hovhaness
    Cantate Domino   Hassler
    Honor and Glory   Bach

	Then Round About the Starrry Throne	Handel
	I will Praise Thee, O Lord	Nystedt
	Jubilate Deo, Omnis terra	Peeters
III:	All Ye Who Music Love	Donato-Greyson
	Aint'a that Good News	Dawson
	Neighbors' Chorus	Offenbach
IV:	Fa Una Canzone	Vecchi
	Now Sing We All this Day	Hassler
	He is Good and Handsome	Pearson-Grayson
	Let All Our Lives be Joyous	Vecchi
	Deh Vieni from Le Nozze di Figaro	Mozart

Karen Ross, soprano

O Occi Manza Mia	di Lasso
O Bella Fusa	di Lasso

The Madrigal Singers

Gypsy in My Soul	arr. Leyden
Man of La Mancha	arr. Warnick

Man of La Mancha, Little Bird, Little Bird, Dulcinea, To Each His Dulcinea, The Impossible Dream

Battle Hymn of the Republic — arr. Ringwald

Kathy Wright and Patti Hord, Accompanists

I chose a great variety of music for the concerts in England. Among the selections were larger works: Schubert's Mass in G, and the music of "Man of La Mancha." I told my students that I didn't want to carry all that music across the ocean, so we worked long hours to memorize all of it. My talented accompanists memorized their parts too. I took music for me – and only for me.

CHAPTER 9:
THE MASON COUNTY YEARS: 1970-74
"Expanding Horizons"

The '70s were rich years for the advancement of choral music in the community. Mason County students continued to attend the music festivals and came back with ratings of superior year after year.

I started a string program in the Mason County Schools and taught violin, viola, cello and bass to a large number of students. The program attracted the support of the Kentucky Arts Commission, the University of Kentucky and the Maysville Community College. Two orchestras were developed: a Concert Orchestra and the Limestone Youth Symphony. The Limestone Youth Orchestra Foundation was formed and the program of string instruction was enriched by the financial support of the Browning Fund and the Elsie and Gordon Lee Downing Fund for the Arts. The latter is an on-going source of support that has enriched the lives of countless young people in this area.

The high school choir attended the Morehead Choral Clinic each year and received instruction from many of the nation's outstanding choral conductors. The High School Concert Choir performed at Morehead State University and the University of Kentucky and spent several days at both institutions in the summer, receiving choral instruction. The choir made two trips to Europe, in 1974 at the invitation of the National Educational Scholarship Foundation, and in 1979 at the invitation of Alexander Giese, president of the Association for International Cultural Exchange, from Kurt Waldheim, Secretary-General of the United Nations and from the President of the Federal Republic of Austria.

I took 33 entries to the music festival at Morehead in the spring of 1970, garnering 30 superiors and three excellents. Robert Myers of Dover, a junior at the high school, was chosen as outstanding soloist of the entire contest. Bobby's selection was "Caro Mio Ben" by Giordani, and I played his accompaniment. Bobby went on to become a very successful high school choral conductor.

Other soloists receiving superior were Mary Ransbottom, Jerry

Zeigler, and Phil Marinaro. Excellents went to the Minerva Girls' Chorus, a girls' trio comprised of Debbie Biddle, Mary Ransbottom and Sharon Murphy, and Michael Marinaro, baritone solo.

In April 1970, Sara Holroyd, director of choral music at the University of Kentucky, visited my school. After hearing the choirs, she invited my boys to join the University Men's Glee Club in a concert. We were thrilled at this opportunity and worked hard on the choral numbers. I conducted the combined men's chorus on "The Last Words of David" by Randall Thompson, and she conducted the rest of the program that also included the University Women's Glee Club. It was a great experience that left an indelible mark on the young singers to always strive for a rich, full sound.

The Spring Concert was held May 11, 1970, and featured a new chorus, the Chorale, a selective group of 35 students whose repertoire included music from the Renaissance to the present. Accompanying this group were Lex Browning, guitar; David Anderson, bass violin; and Paul Hunt, percussion. A highlight of the concert was the presentation of Mozart's "Regina Coeli" by the Concert Choir. Accompanying the choir was the Chamber Orchestra composed of Connie Runyon and Barbara Tubbesing, flute; Jeff Jones and Stockton Wood, trumpet; Paul Hunt, tympani; Rebecca Burke and Mrs. Ronald Haun, violin; and Nancy South, cello. Accompanists on the program were Mary Ransbottom, Henry Jefferson, Jr., and Nancy Hasson. Groups participating included were the 75-member concert choir, the Girls' Chorus of 75, the Boys' Chorus of 65, the Ninth Grade Girls' Chorus of 75, and the Chorale of 35 members.

One of the most exciting experiences for the Mason County Concert Choir was its participation in a concert of polychoral compositions with the Eastern Kentucky University Choir, under the direction of Dr. Bruce Hoagland; the Morehead State University Concert Choir, James Ross Beane, conductor; and the Maysville Community College Concert Choir and the Mason County High School Choir, under my direction.

These choirs presented a magnificent concert on Feb. 12, 1971, at the University of Louisville School of Music for the convention of the Kentucky Music Educators and the American Choral Directors'

Associations. The opening number was Charles Ives' "Psalm 150," scored for eight-part chorus and four-part treble chorus, and conducted by Dr. Hoagland. The second number was "Wie schon leuchtet der Morgenstern" by Praetorius, conducted by Mr. Beane. This work is scored for five solo voices, four-part chorus, instrumental doublings, and continuo. The instruments were stationed within the choral members whose parts were doubled. I conducted Pachelbel's "Magnificat," scored for two antiphonal choirs, soloists, and continuo; and Mendelssohn's "Heilig," written for two antiphonal choirs of eight parts each. The concluding number was Gabrieli's "Jubilate Deo," conducted by Mr. Beane. It is scored for eight-part chorus with brass instrumental doubling.

I prepared my two choruses carefully and we had joint rehearsals with the other choirs. Such an opportunity does not come often to high school students, and I am grateful to Dr. Hoagland, and Mr. Beane for having confidence in my musical ability to prepare these young people for such a great choral happening. The members of the Community College Concert Choir were Ricky Alexander, Gary Bailey, Michael Bolden, Karla Bowles, Connie Brewer, Priscilla Browning, John C. Calvert, Ann Carpenter, Christy Clark, Vicky Collins, Nancy Combs, Vicky Dickens, Beverly Gilbert, Vieda Hesler, Helen Huber, Henry Jefferson, Gordon Jones, Glenn Lowe, Bobby Myers, Carla Osborne, Ann Rice, Sandra Smith, Laura Sparks, Steve Strosnider, Tim Teagarden, Genrose Turner, Winn Turner, Patti Vice, Phil Weber, Pat Stackler, Jerome Zeigler, Lowell Cooper, Ann Thompson, Sue Ellen Kirk, Jeff Worthington, Gary Biddle, and Debbie Biddle.

The members of the Mason County Concert Choir were Lynn Gifford, Eddie Moran, Gary DeVaughan, Terry Cowan, Robert Hay, Chris Browning, Alex Fassolitis, David Anderson, Greg Rosser, Lloyd Schultz, Lynn Todd, Jeff Worthington, Terry Hinson, Debbie Ring, Lolene Soward, Louise Zeigler, Elizabeth Smart, Gwen Jones, Patti Wheeler, Cheryl Smoot, Cindy Biddle, Debbie Burke, Susan Wood, Louanne Hampton, Sherry Barbee, and Jackie Jones.

Without a doubt, the events of March and April 1971 left another indelible mark on all participants. Mr. Joseph Ceo, conductor of the Central Kentucky Youth Orchestra, invited my chorus to join in the presentation of "A German Requiem" by Brahms in Christ the King Church in Lexington. Three years before, in 1968, the Concert Choir had performed with the Youth Orchestra in the Teen Arts Festival. I decided that my college choir should share in this rare opportunity and I trained both groups for this concert. A review in the Lexington Herald of March 29th described it as "one of the most exciting and significant afternoons in the musical history of the community.... A near-capacity crowd was on hand to thrill to the performance.... The exactness of the orchestra, the increasing sonority and great crescendo led to the power and resonance of the full chorus entering at peak intensity with an exclamation of great dramatic impact.... Exquisite in quietness, the music swelled and soared to emotional heights intensified by the physical soaring to the vaulted ceiling, which gave the feeling by being surrounded and enfolded by the sound." We presented the same concert a few days later in Maysville.

The Spring Concert in 1971 included the following program:

Round About the Starry Throne	Handel
How Lovely Is Thy Dwelling Place	Brahms
O Come, Let Us Sing Unto the Lord	Diemer
Concert Choir	
Awake the Harp	Haydn
How Excellent Thy Name	Hanson
Girls' Chorus	
Song of the Gray Goose Feather	Holslag
Battle of Jericho	Bartholomew
Boys' Ensemble	
Keep in the Middle of the Road	Goff
Ride the Chariot	Smith
O, Mary, Don't You Weep	Rhea
Spirate, Pur Spirate	Donaudy
Michael Bolden, soloist	
Marching to Pretoria	Abbott
Boys' Glee Club	
Praise Him	Bach
Cherubic Hymn	Gretchaninoff
My Lord, What a Morning	Wilson

One of Those Songs	Cable
Ninth Grade Girls' Chorus	
Sing We and Chant It	Morley
Il est bel et bon	Passereau
I Attempt From Love's Sickness to Fly	Purcell
Robert Myers, soloist	
Cool Water	Ringwald
Way Down Yonder in New Orleans	Ades
That Old Gang of Mine	Cacavas
Back in Your Own Back Yard	Casey
The Chorale	

E. T. Mullikin, guitar; David Anderson, string bass; Paul Hunt, percussion. Accompanists for the concert were Priscilla Browning and Vieda Hesler.

The first annual concert of the Mason County Middle School was held Dec. 17, 1971, in the new school. Featured on the program was the Limestone Youth Orchestra presenting works by Corelli, Vivaldi, and Hovhaness. Five choruses were heard on the program: the Seventh Grade Girls' Chorus, the Seventh Grade Mixed Chorus, the Eighth Grade Girls' Chorus, the Eighth Grade Mixed Chorus and the Middle School Concert Choir. Priscilla Browning was the accompanist for the choruses and Virginia Browning was my choral assistant. Both young women came to school every day to help me with the music program. I will always be indebted to Percy for her marvelous musicianship and cheerfulness and encouragement. Jinny, too, made my work exceedingly pleasant by being a wonderful teacher's aide. Not only did she come every day to school to help in any way she could, but also she took me to her home for lunch and then returned me back to school. It was a wonderful break for me, and we had plenty of time to make wonderful plans and dream big dreams.

On Feb. 1, 1973, the Concert Choir of Mason County High School presented a concert in the Recital Hall at Morehead State University. Priscilla Browning and I worked hard on the program. We programmed three major works: Haydn's "Te Deum Laudamus," the Vivaldi "Gloria," and Hanson's "Song of Democracy." Many university professors have marveled at the ability of these county kids to master the type of literature we always did. It didn't seem odd to me, for that was what I chose to do all the years I was teaching. Throughout the years, students have written to tell me how much it meant to them to have done this wonderful choral literature.

The choir members at this time were: Kay Adams, Sherry Barbee, Mary Campbell, Georgia Fegan, Betty Fraley, Marla Kalb, Connie Lowe, Marilyn Markwell, Joyce Martin, Debbie McNutt, Mildred smith, Sharon Thomas, Melissa Turner, Paige Vice, Scherrie Wilson, Sandy Adams, Frances Campbell, Elaine Hansen Maria Harrison, Vickie High, Terry Hinson, Debbie Hutchison, Joan Johnson, Karen Jones, Debbie Ring, Elizabeth Smart, Penny Smith, Lolene Soward, Cheri Ward, Carla Whalen, Ann Wood, Louise Zeigler, Jeff Bolden, Henry Campbell, Mark Carpenter, Bill Harrison, Robert Hay, Mickey Lang, Richard Marshall, Rickey Price, Lloyd Schultz, Steven VanCamp, Jeff Worthington, David Anderson, Tim Barker, Christopher Browning, Steve Carlisle, Ricky Clark, Terry Cowan, Jeff Danner, Mark Davis, Mike DeAtley, Gary DeVaughan, Greg Grigson, John Henderson, Jim

Performing at the Capitol in Frankfort, 1974.

Hicks, Greg Hinson, Paul Hunt, Floyd Johnson, Ernie McDowell, Robert Miller, Jeff Newsome, Greg Rosser, Lynn Todd, and Keith Trumbo.

The choir was asked to present a concert in Louisville for the convention of the Kentucky Music Educators Convention. We did so on March 1, 1974. and programmed the Haydn Mass in B-flat and Mozart's "Vesperae solemnes de confessore," with soloists Melissa Turner, Maria Harrison, Terry Heflin, and Christopher Browning. We also sang "The Song of the Open Road" by Dello Joio.

On April 23, 1974, the Concert Choir was invited to do a joint concert with the University Choristers of the University of Kentucky in Lexington. We again sang Haydn's Mass in B Flat, with the same soloists. We joined the University Choristers in presenting three numbers from Mozart's "Vesperae solemnes de confessore."

In a review of this concert, David Browning, music critic for the Lexington Herald, wrote, "the Mason County group is a well trained and musically disciplined choral ensemble." The Haydn "was further enhanced by a solo quartet graced with the secure and very beautiful soprano voice of Melissa Turner and the absolutely stunning alto voice of Maria Harrison. Hearing these two outstanding young voices induces the painful reflection that in recent years the university has failed to produce voices capable of capturing more than momentary interest, much less generating excitement."

Mary Denney, the director of music in the Maysville Schools, suggested we invite Robert Page to come to Maysville and conduct a choral clinic for our combined choruses. We were thrilled when he agreed to come. He was a guest in our home, and we enjoyed the association with him tremendously. At this time he was the head of choral activities at Temple University in Philadelphia. Our students had attended choral clinics he had conducted at Morehead University, and we longed to have our own choral clinic with this outstanding musician. Mr. Page, widely known in the field of music, had conducted all-state groups all over the country. As a soloist he had appeared in leading roles in many operas and musical comedies.

Rehearsals began on a Friday afternoon in November 1974, continued all day on Saturday, and the concert was presented on Sunday in the Maysville High School Auditorium.

The program included the Schubert Mass in G, "Six Chansons" by Hindemith, and Perschetti's "Te Deum." Solo parts in the mass were done by Billie Faye Brierly, soprano, from Mason County; Billy Mearns, tenor, Maysville, and Scott Poe, bass, Maysville.

Members of the chorus from Maysville High were Mary Owen Baber, Libby Clay, Charlotte Case, Dottie Cable, Jane Collins, Edna Gordon, Margaret Igleheart, Rita Osborne, Connie Runyon, Darlene Smith, Earlise Smith, Yvette Smith, Cathy Arnold, Ethel Bothman, Betty Bramel, Angie Case, Ruth Commodore, Marsha Gardner, Vickie Ginn, Sallie Hay, Kathy Haley, Vonnie Hunt, Cynda Kesler, Rhonda LeForge, Patty Nash, Sue Phelps, Sandra Roe, Billie Jo Toncray, Olivia Whyte, Becky Wilcox, Barbara Wilkes, Ramona Vice, Karen Meadows, Billy Godbey, Warren Helvey, Jimmy Manning, Billy Mearns, Terry Simms, Jimmy Richards, Gordon Jones, Bobby Toncray, Terry Heflin, David Landreth, David Brewer, Jerry Fleming, Bobby Mattingly, Bobby McDonald, Tommy Morris, Scottie Poe, Jerry Hetrick, Ronnie Merrill, Larry Hesler, and Denny Tarbin.

Members of the chorus from Mason County were Billie Brierley, Melanie Humphries, Jeannine Mains, Connie Bridges, Pam Whaley, Lenora Wallingford, Linda Ensor, Lyde Worthington, Sue Cropper, Priscilla Clark, Pam White, Karen Ross, Annie Dugan, Janet Mason, Nancy King, Debbie King, Carol Cracraft, Debbie Botkins, Cherry Reed, Ann Parker, Lois Hord, Mary E. Cooper, Jackie Curtis, Betty Lowe Verville, Kay Burke, Jennifer Thompson, Donna Roberson, Pattie Hord, Sara Vice, Peggy Hendricks, Kathy Porter, Connie Robinson, Kathy Wright, Libby Clary, Connie Sapp, Mickey Wallingford, Carol Chumbler, Jo Ann Henderson, Lois Howell, Debbie Lawler, Jean Bryant, Barbara Morton, Martha Fox, Jerry Dempsey, Danny Jones, Charles Dieterich, Joey Finn, Dennis Dunaway, David Grigson, Kenneth Roberts, Marvin Maynard, Gary Biddle, Paul Mullikin, Billy Boyd, Ricky Alexander, Tommy Hinton, Charles Calvert, David Dillon, John Marshall, James Crawford, Marc Woodward, Gary DeVaughan, Robert Jones, Eldon Jordan, Bill Wheat, Pat Hartley, Kenneth Chamblin, Darrell Clayton, and Larry Hickman.

In November 1973, I received a telegram from the National

Educational Scholarship Foundation announcing that my choir had been invited to participate in the International Association for Cultural Exchange to be held in Vienna, Austria, in July of 1974. The Mason County High School Concert Choir was one of 90 to be nominated and one of the nine chosen to take part in the Vienna Festival for Youth and Music. The artistic director of the choral festival was Dr. Lara Hoggard, internationally known choral conductor and head of choral activities at the University of North Carolina at Chapel Hill. Dr. Hoggard had telephoned to say that a panel of judges had selected my choir in a session held at the University of New Mexico at Albuquerque. A determining factor was that in the past spring my students had earned 30 superiors out of 30 entries in the music festival. The choruses seeking nomination had come from universities, colleges, and high schools throughout the nation. Other groups selected included the Amarillo High School Bel Canto Choir from Amarillo, Texas; the Mihai Viteazul choir from Bucharest, Romania; the Master Singers of Glenbrook, Illinois; the Gregory Portland High School Choir of Gregory, Texas; the Robert E. Lee High School Chorale, Midland, Texas; the Oshkosh West High A Cappella Choir, Oshkosh, Wisconsin; the Needham B. Broughton Choral Ensemble, Raleigh, North Carolina; and the South Haven High

Kalverienbad Kirche, Vienna.

School Choir, South Haven, Michigan.

Shortly after receiving the invitation to participate, the parents of the students held several meetings where plans were made to make the trip possible. Many fund-raising activities took place, and I was overwhelmed at the generosity of the community. An auction was held at Kachler's Auction House in Mayslick with many donated items sold, including an autographed Ray Harm print, a square grand piano, an antique love seat, an antique arm chair, a record player, and a Bendix home ironer. All donations were tax deductible and the proceeds went to the Choir Fund.

A concert was presented in the Maysville High School Auditorium in which Lyda Lewis, Maysville's Miss Kentucky of 1974, the Marlin Family, and the Concert Choir performed. Clyde Barbour, local owner of Super Value Stores, was responsible for the event, and his energy, enthusiasm, and financial support will be long remembered in this community.

Governor Wendell Ford and his staff graciously received us when we arrived at the capitol in Frankfort for a performance on March 12, 1974. We sang "Heilig" for double choir by Mendelssohn, "Hodie Nobis Caelorum Rex" by Mozart, "Blessing, Glory, and Wisdom" by Bach; "I Will Praise Thee, O Lord" by Nystedt, "Laudate Dominum" by Mozart, with Melissa Turner as soprano soloist, "Ain't-a That Good News" by Dawson, and "Song of the Open Road" by Dello Joio, with Rick Illman on trumpet.

Many compliments were received by the audience that gathered in the balconies of this majestic rotunda of the state capitol. We were taken to the House of Representatives and the Senate where we were introduced and given the appointment and commission to be "Kentucky's Ambassadors of Good Will." We were then escorted to the Governor's Mansion where we enjoyed a luncheon. I was proud of my students for their lovely manners and gracious demeanor in this great happening in their lives.

Governor Ford sent a check for $5,000 in token of appreciation of the honor that the choir has brought to the commonwealth in being chosen to represent Kentucky at the festival. This letter stated, "Along with the enclosure the governor wishes you a successful and happy trip and he is sending you some of the state's sterling cuff links to present as gifts to the various mayors and dignitaries representing the cities you will be visiting." Lt. Governor Julian Carroll wrote a letter of congratulations saying, "Yours is a coveted recognition and one that brings distinction to your school, your community, and the Commonwealth. Again I commend all of you and feel unusual pride in knowing how ably we will be represented at the European performances. I know yours will be a meaningful and enjoyable trip."

As a tribute to Kentucky, and the choir, Dr. Lara Hoggard, the Vienna Festival's artistic director, wrote a special choral arrangement of "My Old Kentucky Home," to be sung at the Festival. It is dedicated to me.

In May 1974 Lara Hoggard came to Maysville to conduct a two-day workshop for the choir to prepare us for our trip. I had first met him when I attended several choral workshops sponsored by the University of Kentucky. He had been the director of these sessions, and we had become good friends. He worked with my students to put the finishing touches on Orff's "Carmina Burana," that they would perform with other choirs in Vienna. He rehearsed with the choir on Thursday and Friday, and on Friday evening the choral parents gave a dinner in his honor at the Middle School and present were all chaperones, choir members and parents.

On April 3, 1974, the University of Kentucky Choristers, conducted by Sara Holroyd, came to Maysville to present a concert in the Maysville High School Auditorium. I entertained the choir with a dinner at the Maysville Country Club before the concert, and upon leaving for the auditorium I noticed how strangely still the atmosphere was. The concert had just started when Dr. Harry Denham interrupted to say we should all take cover, as a tornado was approaching rapidly. I took the responsibility to break down the door to the basement of the high school building, and the U.K. choir took refuge there for the night. All of us later rushed to our respective homes and went to our basements to wait out the storm. The small town of Dover, near Maysville, was demolished, as were some houses on Jersey Ridge. The University Choir left the next morning when an "All Clear" was sounded. It was quite an experience!

On April 26, 1974, I took the choir to St. Louis where we participated in a contest the Six Flags over Mid-America's Third Annual Choral Festival. We sang "Awake the Harp" by Haydn, "Ave Maria" by Rachmaninoff; and "Jubilate Deo Omnis Terra" by Peters. We rated superior! After the contest we had dinner on the Huckleberry Finn steamer and enjoyed a trip up the Mississippi River. Virginia and Larry Browning, former Maysville residents who had moved to St. Louis, met us at the boat dock and we enjoyed being with them. After dinner, the students entertained other passengers with a spontaneous program of piano playing and singing.

The parents and students worked very hard to raise money for the trip. I was amazed and humbled at the outpouring of financial help from the many organizations in Maysville. The banks, the City Commission, and the County Commission were generous in their contributions and the Browning Family fund saw that no student would be left behind. At last the day arrived for our trip to Cincinnati to begin our adventure. We were greeted at the airport by personnel from American Airlines, and when we boarded the plane the pilot asked if I would arrange a concert as we neared New York, where we would board a Pam Am plane for Vienna. The choir gathered in the rear of the plane and performed for the other passengers. The plane had to circle New York for nearly

Rathaus, Vienna.

an hour, so the concert went on and on! There was much applause from our fellow travelers and best wishes.

When our plane landed at the Vienna airport, we were met by Dr. Hoggard and two adorable Austrian children, dressed in traditional Austrian outfits, who presented me with a bouquet of flowers. After checking in at our hotel, we discovered that many of the students were without luggage. I went to the airlines office in the city and was told they could purchase the necessary items needed at a large department store. The lost baggage arrived the following day – it had gone on to New Zealand!

On registering at our hotel in Vienna, I was given a note from Mrs. Laurence Browning that she and her son had flown on ahead and were at the Bristol Hotel. She wanted to surprise me and welcome me to Vienna. She invited my daughter, Connie, and me for tea at her hotel the following day. She and her son Robert also attended the opening concert.

The opening ceremonies were held on a stage in front of the Rathausplatz in which the mayor and other dignitaries welcomed the choruses, bands, and orchestras to Vienna. We performed several numbers with the chorus in formal dress. Later we had supper in the restaurant there, and strolling violinists serenaded us at our table,

Early in the week we attended a concert in the grand hall in the Schonbrunn Schloss. We sat in the very same hall where Mozart as a child had performed for the emperor and empress. The room is gorgeous with many, many mirrors and chandeliers; gold and ocher were the predominant colors.

We participated in a mass in a nearby church. We had been asked to sing a mass a cappella and I had prepared one in Latin. The priest intoned the mass in German, and we responded in Latin. It made for a very interesting service, indeed. A burial ground was in front of the church, and we were amazed to see pictures of the deceased on the tombstones. Our next concert was given at Schloss Rosenau in a ballroom of the castle and we were guests for a luncheon there.

The choirs gave individual performances in Vienna before a panel of international adjudicators, gave performances in different locations, and joined together in the presentation of Orff's "Carmina Burana" and the Duruflé Requiem. The nine choirs met for the first time in rehearsals in the huge hall of the Vienna International Garden Show. My students had been assigned to do the "Carmina Burana" and we were well prepared for the first rehearsal. Dr. Hoggard was the conductor and the Pisek Chamber Orchestra from Pisek, Czechoslovakia, provided the accompaniment. All instructions from the conductor to the orchestra had to be given through an interpreter.

Two of my students, Melissa Turner and Maria Harrison, were selected to participate in a solo competition. The jury was composed of Jiri Chvala, Czechoslovakia; Lara Hoggard; and Gunther Theuring, Austria. I shall never forget the joy and excitement when it was announced that Melissa Turner had won first place! The prize was a year's scholarship to a school of her choice. She chose the University of Cincinnati's College-Conservatory of Music. The judges remarked on the incredible beauty of Melissa's legato line. It was one of my greatest experiences in teaching to have her in junior high, high school, and church choirs. Her mother, Genrose Swango Turner, possessed a gorgeous soprano voice, and was a valued soloist and member of all my civic chorus, church and college choirs, and now of the Limestone Chorale. Melissa's father, Winn, has a wonderful tenor voice, and he has been a valued member of the many choruses I have conducted. He first gained "stardom" when he played the part of The Frog" in "Grandmother's Flower Garden" when I taught at Orangeburg – the only operetta I have ever done.

While preparing for the trip to Vienna, I had received a telephone call from Mrs. Robert Asher of the National Educational Scholarship Foundation, saying that my choir had been chosen to do a special concert in Furstenfeld located in southern Austria. The mayor of the town presented me with pictures of the region, and I thanked him in German. I had practiced my "speech" all the way down on the bus. The guide assigned to our group was a very personable young lady who was a fourth-year student in the Medical School of the University of Vienna and she helped me with my short talk.

The program given is Furstenfeld was well received, and a crowd of people tried to talk to me in German! Many indicated that they, too, sang in choirs and they mentioned the "Carmina Burana" over and over. I needed a trumpeter for the Dello Joio "Song of the Open Road." I was provided one and he proved to be a delight to all of us. He was Uno Kolme of the Cologne Symphony Orchestra. We had quite a time understanding each other when we met in our hotel in Vienna to practice the music. He could not speak English, and my German was dreadful. We managed to communicate through musical terms! This is the program we presented: "Ostereichische Bundeshymne" by Mozart, "Song of the Open Road by Dello Joio; "All Ye Who Music Love" by Donato; "Fa Una Canzone" by Vecchi; "In-a That Great Gittin' Up Morning" arranged by Foltz, with Connie Lowe, Soprano; "Ain't a That Great News" Dawson; Selections from "My Fair Lady" by Lowe; "Gypsy in My Soul" by Boland, "Hope for the Future" by Strommen, "Oklahoma" by Rogers, "That Old Gang of Mine" by Cacavas, "Choose Something Like a Star" by Thompson; "Neighbors' Chorus" by Offenbach; "Song of Democracy" by Hanson; "My Old Kentucky Home" by Foster, arranged by Hoggard, with Melissa Turner and Maria Harrison, soloists; "Osterreich, Gute Nach, Auf Widersehen" arranged by Hoggard.

The members of the choir were: Kay Adams, Dorothy Browning, Elizabeth Browning, Virginia Browning, Marla Kalb, Connie Lowe, Debbie McNutt, Perri Moore, Mildred Smith, Sharon Thomas, Melissa Turner, Paige Vice, Sherrie Wilson, Janet Allen, Karen Crockett, Patti Grigson, Elaine Hansen, Maria Harrison, Jane Holland, Donna Jefferson, Joan Johnson, Sharon Johnson, Marilyn Markell, Leslie Sapp, Penny Smith, Brenda Thomas, Pam Tolle, Harry Campbell, Steve Carlisle, Mark Carpenter, Terry Heflin, Jimmy Likins, Jeff Silvey, Robert Thomas, Christopher Browning, Keith Browning, Kelly Fritz, Jim Hicks, C. J. Hunter, Don Jefferson, Michael Jefferson, Kelly Kalb, Jeff Newsome, and Russ Tolle. The chaperones were John Branson, the principal of Mason County High School, Laura Branson, Priscilla Browning, Virginia Browning, Lucille Grigson, Ben Lowe, Harold Runyon, Connie Runyon, and Alpha Straub.

To visit Vienna is a joyful experience, but to perform in the city of the Muses, the capital of Music, has a transforming effect. I thought about how exciting it was for our group of choristers and chaperones from a small town in Kentucky to be a small part of the hypnotic charm of this dynamic city where the zest for living and beauty were all about us. Everywhere there are reminders of the great musicians who left their mark there: Mozart, Strauss, Beethoven. Our first concert in the church where Schubert worshipped was an overwhelming experience. Attending the concert in Schonbrunn Palace made me feel like we had slipped back into time and were a part of the grandeur and glitter of baroque magnificence. A rare experience was the trip to the Vienna State Opera in the Ringstrasse, where we were asked to perform a few numbers with many tourists looking on and applauding. I will always remember the visit to the Stadtpark where the statue of Johann Strauss, the Waltz King, presides over the dance floor and girls in white flowing dresses dance to the orchestra's playing the famous waltzes. We sat a small round tables eating ice cream, and I too danced a waltz with one of my students.

High above the city are the spires of Stephansdom, the Gothic hallmark of Vienna. When we toured that cathedral I yearned to give a concert there. I did not know in 1974 that I would be asked to do that very thing in 1979. I was moved by the woodcarvings in the cathedral and particularly the ones done of the apostles centuries ago. The huge pipe organ in the rear balcony appears to be held in place by cherubim.

We visited one of the many houses where Beethoven lived, and the students visited the Wurstelprater Park and rode on the Giant Ferris Wheel there.

We took a sightseeing tour that brought us through the Brenner Pass in the Dolomite Mountains in northern Italy. After lunch on the terrace of a small hotel, the students were taken up to a glacier while Alpha Straub and I found a projecting rock, high in the Alps. There we sat and looked at all the splendor of those breathtaking mountains. When we noticed a small band of children being led down the slope by a nun, we followed and entered a very small chapel, nestled in the mountains.

In Salzburg we visited the Mozarteum, and traveled up the cog railway to the top of the mountain. We then went on to Innsbruck where we spent a few days. Our hotel was on the top of a mountain and overlooked the valley. We gave a concert, then traveled to the Munich airport for the flight home.

Chapter 10:
The Mason County Years: 1975-82
"Third Time's A Charm"

A great sorrow and personal loss to me was the death of my husband, Harold E Runyon, in January 1975. We had enjoyed 32 years of a very happy marriage. He was a great source of strength and encouragement to me in my endeavors. Our two children, Randolph Paul and Constance Coralie, were a constant pride and joy to us; they have fulfilled the ambitions we shared for them.

I have never been prone to quit the task I am engaged in, though, so I continued my work with the Mason County Schools, the Community College, the church and the community.

The choral and string programs at Mason County Schools continued to prosper and thrive. On December 17, 1974, the strings presented a concert in the band room under the direction of Miss Barbara Hodges, who had joined the faculty of the Mason County Schools as a string instructor. She was a graduate of the University of Cincinnati College-Conservatory of Music, a talented violinist and a member of the Lexington Philharmonic Orchestra. Schools participating in the program included Mayslick, Washington, Minerva, Orangeburg, Straub Elementary, and the Middle School.

The high school string quartet, composed of Karen Jones, Sharon Thomas, Marla Wilson and Elaine Henson, performed the "Rondo" from Quartet No. 2 by Haydn. Karen Jones also performed the Concerto in E Minor by Nardini. Other soloists taking part were Joan Sapp, cello, and Mark Hook, violin. The High School Orchestra played "Rondo" by Purcell and "Yuletide Fantasy" by Mueller. It was satisfying to see that our string program had grown so much in such a short time that a full-time teacher had been employed.

The program of the spring concert of May 8, 1975, shows the maturity of the high school choral department:

Dixit Dominus from	
Vesperae solemnes de confessore	Mozart
Vere Languores	Victoria

Magnificat	Buxtehude

    Barbara Hodge, Karen Jones, Sharon Thomas, violins;
    Marla Wilson, viola; Elaine Hansen, cello; Priscilla
    Browning, harpsichord
    The Concert Choir

Now God Be Praised	Vulpius
Keep An Eye On Me	Gustafson
Make A Joyful Noise Unto God	Handel
Thou Who Wast God	Davis

    The Ninth Grade Chorus

Pueri Hebraeorum (for double choir)	Thompson
Un moto di gioa from "The Marriage of Figaro"	Mozart

    Marla Wilson, soprano

Laudi alla Vergine Maria	Verdi

    The Advanced Girls' Chorus

With A Voice of Singing	Shaw
Sebben Crudele	Caldara

    Kelly Fritz, baritone

Hop Up, My Ladies	Gilbert

    The Male Quartet

Stopping By Woods on a Snowy Evening	Thompson

    The Boys' Glee Club

Sweet Love Doth Now Invite	Dowland
O Bella Fusa	di Lasso
O Mio Babino Caro	Puccini

    Marla Kalb, soprano

Fair Maid, Thy Loveliness	Hassler
In These Delightful Pleasant Groves	Purcell

    The Chamber Singers

Gloria	Poulenc

    Gloria, Laudamus Te, Domine Deus, Domine fili
    unigenite, Domine Deus, Agnus Dei, Qui sedes,
Marla Kalb, soprano
The Concert Choir
Once again, the Concert Choir was asked to present a concert

at Morehead State University. On Wednesday, March 3, 1976, we performed this program of difficult works: Motet V, "Come, Jesus, Come" by Bach; "Song of Fate" by Brahms; "Vere Languores" by Victoria; "Laude alla Vergine Maria" by Verdi; "Ave Mari" by Rachmaninoff; and "Gloria" by Poulenc.

The four choruses from the high school all received unanimous superiors at the contest held in April 1976, at Morehead. The Freshmen Mixed Chorus of 50 voices sang "Alleluia" by Bach and "Praise to the Lord" by Hokansen. The Girls' Chorus of 40 voices sang "How Lovely Is Thy Dwelling Place" by Brahms and "Laudi alla Vergine Maria" by Verdi. The Boys' Glee Club of 35 voices sang "Let There Be Music" by Williams and Smith's "Ride the Chariot." The numbers for the High School Choir were "Awake the Harp" by Haydn and Rachmaninoff's "Ave Maria." After this choir sang there was a standing ovation, including the three judges!

The Spring Concert of May of 1976 was held at the Opera Theater on May 18, and the program featured an unusual and fine number: "Gloria" by John Zeigler. John was a member of the choir, and since he was in junior high school he had been writing music. He was deeply engrossed in the Baroque period of music history. I taught classes in

theory and music history both at the high school and at the community college. I knew John was talented, so I arranged for an appointment with the head of the composition department of the University of Kentucky and took him to Lexington for the interview. The professor assured me that what he was doing showed promise. John received a scholarship to Morehead and continued writing music. He has a beautiful tenor voice, and is one of the finest choral members I have ever had. I taught him viola in our classes before school, and he is a valued member of the Limestone Adult Chamber Orchestra. He is also the director of the Chancel Choir at the First Christian Church, my former post.

On this program I presented music from the Broadway play, "Oliver," by Lionel Bart.

On December 19, 1976, the Fine Arts Department of Mason County High School presented a Christmas Festival that featured the choruses, band, and art department. The High School Choir sang the "Missa Sancti Nicolai" by Haydn and, in a lighter vein, "The Night Before Christmas" by Simeone.

At the music festival in the spring of 1977 all four choruses – the Freshman Chorus, the Boys Glee Club, the Girls' Chorus, and the Concert Choir – not only received unanimous superior ratings, but also a standing ovation. Other superior ratings were given the following groups: three mixed quartets, three mixed ensembles, two boys' ensembles, a boys' quartet, a girls' ensemble, a madrigal group,

Performance, 1972.

and eight vocal solos.

In May 1977 I inaugurated a Fine Arts Festival in which the chorus, orchestras, soloists, young composers, and art students were included. The opening event was a choral concert with Peter Gharabian as guest conductor. Mr. Gharabian, head of the Dana School of Music in Wellesley, Massachusetts, conducted Mozart's "Regina Coeli."

At 3 p.m. on the opening day of the festival an art show headed by Mrs. James Werline, high school art teacher, was held in the lobby of the high school field house. At 4 p.m. the orchestra played in the band room. Featured were the Concert Orchestra, composed of students from grades 2-9, and the Chamber Orchestra, composed of high school students.

On Wednesday a vocal recital and original student compositions of both choral and instrumental compositions were performed. The young composers featured on this program were John Zeigler, Tim Marinaro, and Richard Blake.

The concluding concert in the Fine Arts Festival was given on June 8, when the Limestone Youth Orchestra performed Beethoven's Symphony No. 1.

On May 6, 1978 the choirs, ensembles and soloists received 17 superior and two excellent ratings at the contest in Morehead. Superiors were awarded to the Male Quartet, which sang "Do You Fear the Wind"; the Boys' Ensemble, "King Jesus is A-Listening"; the Madrigal Group, "In These Delightful, Pleasant Groves" by Purcell; the Girls' Ensemble, "Come, Let Us Start a Joyful Song; the Ninth Grade Boys' Ensemble, "Good News," arranged by Smith; the Beginning Chorus, "Alleluia" by Bach and "Gloria" by Vivaldi; the High School Boys' Chorus, "Hallelujah, Amen" by Handel and "Shenandoah," arranged by Bartholomew; the Girls' Chorus, "Agnus Dei" by Mozart and "Go, Lovely Rose" by Quilter; the High School Choir, "Quoniam" by Haydn and "Vere Languores" by Vittoria; Richard Blake, for the vocal solo "Honor and Arms" by Handel; Debi Nichols, "Alma del Core" by Caldara; Carla Wilson, "Tu Lo Sai" by Durante; Kelly Kalb, "Invictus" by Hahn; John Zeigler, "Would You Gain the Tender Creatures"; Timothy Marinaro, "Spirate, Pur Spirate" by Danaudy; Roy Ritchie, "Sing Me a Chanty' by Wellesly. Excellent ratings went to Penny

Grigson, for the soprano solo "Alma del Core" by Caldara, and to the Mixed Ninth Grade Ensemble.

On May 15, 1978, my choral and instrumental groups at the high school presented a series of concerts. The first program on Monday night featured the Mixed Chorus, the Girls Chorus, and the Boys Glee Club. The Mixed Chorus presented "Neue Liebeslieder" by Brahms comprising 15 love songs sung in German. Soloists were Elizabeth Browning, a freshman at Carnegie-Mellon University; Carla Wilson, Debi Nichols, and John Zeigler, all seniors at Mason County High School; and Richard Blake, a sophomore. Priscilla Browning and John L. Clarke played the four-hand piano accompaniment. On Wednesday, May 17, a string program was presented featuring the beginning orchestra and the high school chamber orchestra. The high school string quartet performed Mozart's "Quartet in C Major." Another concert featured my voice students and original compositions of John Zeigler and Tim Marinaro.

In the fall of 1978, the Mason County Concert Choir participated in a Festival of Song at the invitation of Dr. Carl Smith, Director of Choral Music at Kentucky State University, Frankfort. The choir performed in the Recital Hall of the University, after which we were guests for luncheon at the president's home on the campus. On Sunday the choir presented an anthem at the First Christian Church

In my choir room, 1978.

in Frankfort, after which they joined the Kentucky State University Choir and other choirs in a performance of Handel's "Messiah" at the Frankfort Sports and Convention Center.

On March 1, 1979, the Mason County Concert Choir joined the University Concert Choir of Morehead State University in a concert that included "Adoramus Te" by Palestrina, "Kyrie Eleison" by Victoria, "Ascendit Deus" by Gallus and the "Requiem" by Duruflé.

The Spring Concert on May 17, 1979, featured several soloists and various ensembles in addition to the choruses:

Te Deum	Haydn
The Concert Choir	
Awake the Harp	Haydn
The Girls Chorus	
Spirate, Pur Spirate	Danaudy
Renita Rosser	
Alma del Core	Caldara
Judy Robinson	
Sing We and Chant It	Morley
The Madrigal Singers	
Vittorio mio Caro	Carissimi
Kent Kalb	
Would You Gain the Tender Creature	Handel
Doug McClanahan	
O Bella Fusa	di Lasso
The Mixed Ensemble	
Song of the Jolly Roger	Chundleigh-Harris
The Boys' Glee Club	
Sing Me a Chanty	Wellesley
Bob McHugh	
A-Rovin	arr. Luboff
The Boys' Ensemble	
O Mary, Don't You Weep	arr. Rice
The Boys' Quartet	
Fraudvoll und Liedvoll	Beethoven
Richard Blake	
Song of Peace	Persichetti

I Will Praise Thee, O Lord	Nystedt
Vere Languores	Vittoria
A Jubilant Song	Dello Joio
The Concert Choir	

The Christmas Concert on December 16, 1979, presented the following numbers:

Psalm 100 (for double choir)	Schutz
Alma Redemptori Mater	Palestrina
Lo, How a Rose E'er Blooming	Praetorius
Lay Down Your Staffs, O Shepherds	Old French Carol
Ave Maria	Rachmaninoff
Heilig (for double choir)	Mendelssohn
Elijah	Mendelssohn

Richard Blake, baritone; Mary Robinson, soprano; Robert Roe, tenor; Judy Robinson, soprano; John Zeigler, tenor; Renita Rosser, mezzo-soprano; Becky Tollner, contralto; Priscilla Browning and Kim Sherdin, piano

One of the most important things in developing an excellent high school choral program is the work done with the middle school. When I first taught in the Mason County Schools I only taught the high school choruses. I supervised the other elementary schools and had teachers for the junior high areas. As time went on, I insisted that I teach them all. After much persuasion, my superintendent, Mr. Hubert Hume, relented and allowed me to teach them all. It was quite a task to cover the entire county, but I managed to do it. When the Middle School was built next to the high school, the job was a lot easier, for they were at last in one building instead of scattered all around the county. I was constantly on the lookout for the young voice that had a special quality. When I found such, I would tell the parents that I would like for this young person to come to my after-school classes. I always taught voice to anyone who wanted to learn the rudiments of singing. My method was to have the middle school student to "sit on the stool" while he or she watched and listened while I taught the older students. This method worked wonders in the development of musicianship in the students.

chapter ten

When they appeared physically ready I began the voice training of the "stool brigade."

By working with the 7th and 8th grades in each school, I was able to develop girls' and boys' ensembles, quartets, madrigal groups, girls' choruses, boys' choruses, and mixed choruses. I took these junior high groups to music contests, and they constantly received the rating of superior. One year, I took the 225-member All-County Junior High Chorus to the contest. I had to take risers to accommodate the large group and the contest had to move to a larger auditorium to hear the group. One judge announced that "history has been made this day with this junior high chorus." Those in charge of the contest each year would tell me that they dreaded "Runyon Day," for I had so many entries. I needed a large suitcase to carry all the contest music. I always had competent and excited student teachers to help with the ordeal. Many parents also attended the contests, and it was a great experience for all.

Over the signature of Prof. Dr. Alexander Giese, President of the Association for International Cultural Exchange, an invitation was extended to me that read: "On behalf of the Honorary Patrons of the World Youth Festival of Music and the Performing Arts, Secretary General of the United Nations, Kurt Waldheim, and the President of the Federal Republic of Austria, Rudolf Kirchschlager, it gives us great pleasure to extend this special invitation to the Mason County

I receive a check from Governor Carroll, right, for our 1979 European trip. Representative Pete Worthington is at the left. (Taken at Caproni's Restaurant in Maysville.)

High School Concert Choir to represent the state of Kentucky at the Inauguration Ceremony of the United Nations International Office Center, the United Nations City, on August 29, 1979 in Vienna, Austria. Your group has been selected by the producer for the sponsoring organization, the Association for International Cultural Exchange to participate in the eighth International Youth and Music Festival as a representative of the United States. This invitation is extended to you in recognition of the high degree of excellence by your group as witnessed by your group's reputation."

I was thrilled to be invited back to Vienna and called a meeting of the parents immediately. At that meeting they were unanimous in their approval of accepting the invitation and Mrs. Donna Hatton was named chairman of the Choir Parents Organization to raise funds for the trip.

The Kentucky's 1979 General Assembly issued a joint resolution designating the choir as the official Kentucky High School Concert Choir to represent the state at the ceremonies. The choir members, chaperones, and I were designated good will ambassadors in our appearances and travels.

We were also asked by the Kentucky Department of Tourism, which had a European Office in Brussels, Belgium, to do additional concerts under their auspices. Two of these would celebrate the 1000th anniversary of the founding of Brussels. We also accepted an invitation from the Mayor of Monaco to present a concert in Monte Carlo.

The moneymaking projects went ahead with great speed. The banks of Maysville contributed sizable amount; the City of Maysville gave $1,000 and Clyde Barbour presented the choir with a check for $2,000. I had a telephone call from a friend who wanted to remain anonymous to tell me that no student would be left behind; she would see that each person was able to make the trip. The Kroger Company sponsored a contest, selling tickets for $2; the winner would have a free shopping spree in the store. Chances were sold on a moped and the winner was Randy Gin of West Third Street. On May 18, Governor Julian Carroll came to Maysville and presented me with a check for $12,000 to be used for the trip. Choir members were asked to raise money in various ways of their choice and I kept a record of each student's earnings. After it was all completed the entire amount needed was raised.

In the June 29, 1979 issue of the Cincinnati Enquirer, columnist Jack Higgins wrote:

Singers Bloom in Maysville; Is it the Water?

Perhaps it's something in the water here, which produces quality-singing voices.

Rosemary Clooney and other members of her family warbled their first notes in these parts, and more recently it's the Mason County High School Concert Choir, which has gained fame. At present the choir is preparing for its third European tour in the past 11 years.

Some 40 youngsters will give Brussels, Belgium, Vienna, Austria, and other cities a taste of Kentucky talent and personality beginning in mid-August. Heading the tour will be Coralie Runyon, the choir's conductor, who took the Mason Countians to England in 1968 and Austria in 1974.

Maybe more than the water or the charm of their hometown, the Maysville–area singers do what they do well enough to be invited to Europe because of Mrs. Runyon. Named the outstanding woman of Kentucky by the University of Kentucky Women's Association in 1971, she has been teaching choral music at Mason County for nearly 20 years.

Not only have her students broadened their horizons through travel, but also association with Mrs. Runyon has inspired a number of them to pursue music careers. Among the latter is Melissa Turner, who has a leading role in the outdoor production, "The Stephen Foster Story," at Bardstown, and Sharon Thomas, a violinist, who recently completed her student teaching with Mrs. Runyon.

Turner and Thomas were on the 1974 trip and are graduate students at the University of Kentucky.

The concert tours are more than just a trip abroad to sing. "If I thought they didn't have a great impact, I wouldn't do it. Anyone can go to Europe," Mrs. Runyon declares.

The impact to which she refers is felt by the singers and

listeners and all Mason Countians with an interest in music, their youngsters and their community.

The Kentucky youngsters have a once-in-a-lifetime experience of singing in some of the hallowed concert halls and cathedrals of Europe, as well as the chance to mingle with their peers from around the world. The home folks, both parents and the community in general, have the vicarious pride of the youngsters' accomplishments.

European audiences, of course, see and hear a worthy group of goodwill ambassadors – some of the best Kentucky and the United States have to offer.

Community pride of the Maysville area is evidenced by the support given the choir. Funds for all the trips were readily raised, prompting Mrs. Runyon to remark "This is a very giving town. There are philanthropic people who care about everything."

Though the choir's repertoire includes show tunes, the effort is to present major musical works. At a United Nations ceremony on Vienna's Danube Plaza, for example, the rendition will be the final movement of Beethoven's Ninth Symphony.

Some of the singers who made the European trips in 1968 and 1974 shared their experiences recently with those preparing for the coming journey. The recurring theme was that the sojourn will be fun, unforgettable, a source of pride and a lot of hard work.

"It wasn't only an educational experience – it was fun. It was a lot of work, but something that stays with you for years after," remarked Turner.

Charles Calvert, a Maysville insurance man and veteran of the 1968 trip, joked that it all happened back when he was young. It gave him a super sense of pride, he stressed, closing a program before an English audience with "The Star Spangled Banner" and "God Save the Queen."

Rick Alexander, who also made the trip and is presently a member of the Mason County Board of Education, was among those who cautioned current choir members, Phillip Grigson

chapter ten

and Judy Robinson, that the frills of home, such as ice in your soft drink, aren't readily available in Europe.

But a few inconveniencies are a small price to pay when the rural and small town kids from Kentucky consider the experiences in store for them. It should be enough to make them break out in song.

I assigned special duties to various chaperones: Denny Keller was in charge of apparel for the choir; Mary Louise ("Hula") Duke was in charge of the gifts to be presented to various dignitaries; and Eula Fowler was appointed my hair dresser, and she took her job very seriously! The State of Kentucky gave us a special discount to purchase navy blue blazers, vests, skirts, pants, and neck scarves, and a duffel bag with the Kentucky Horse Park logo. We were also given Kentucky pins to give to newfound friends in Europe.

The choir looked nice in their outfits for travel, concerts, and sightseeing. The official travel dress for the girls was navy blazer, navy skirt, white blouse, vest, navy shoes, and a Kentucky scarf. For the boys: navy blazer, white shirt, Kentucky tie, grey pants, black shoes, and black socks. For the concert in Monaco: Girls: identical white formals, white sandals, and small button pearl earrings; Boys: black tux, black shoes, and black socks. For concerts in the cathedrals, the choir wore their robes.

It was Mary Louise Duke's responsibility to carry the bourbon that had been labeled with the names of various dignitaries. She soon got help from other chaperones who volunteered to carry the bottles in their duffle bags.

When we boarded the American Airlines plane in Cincinnati for the trip to New York, the pilot asked if I would give a concert on the plane before landing. We did and the passengers were gracious in their compliments. The head stewardess presented me with a bag of miniature bottles of various liquors as thanks for doing the concert! When we arrived in Brussels we were escorted to an area in the large airport where we were welcomed to Belgium, and each person was given a small shiny bag with various samples of Belgian products: chocolates, beef jerky, cheeses, and Napoleon brandy! I told the chaperones to carry the brandy in their duffle bags, and the students were glad not to be bothered with it. After a few days, the students wanted to pour the brandy down the drain and keep the bottles for souvenirs. The chaperones complied!

We were met at the airport by our tour bus and guide assigned to us for our three-week stay in Europe, Louis Polsterer. We arrived in Paris on August 15 and had a marvelous stay there, visiting all the landmarks: the Eiffel Tower, Arc de Triomphe, Notre Dame, Moulin Rouge, Montmartre, and the Latin Quarter, as well many other places. A service was in progress at Notre Dame and the music was glorious. The choir and organ were magnificent.

Several of us went by train to Versailles: Mary Louise Duke, Eula Fowler, Jean Smoot, Doug McClanahan, Suzanne Hinton, Philip Grigson, Connie and I. We had quite an adventure finding our way, but Connie's high school French and hand gestures helped. Versailles is a beautiful city and the grounds around the palace are gorgeous. Unfortunately the palace was closed by the time we arrived, but we enjoyed our trip nonetheless.

The trip through France to Monaco was beautiful. I gave the students assignments: asking them what countries were adjacent to France and for what certain cities were famous. I was appalled at the lack

Singing in Innsbruck.

of geography in their education. They took the assignments seriously and turned in their answers. We arrived at Monte Carlo at night and the trip down the winding Alpine road was frightening to many. It was exciting to see the beautiful Mediterranean Sea! The Kellers – Denny, Carolanne, Caroline and Dennison – were there to meet us at our hotel. They had gone to Europe earlier.

The concert was held at the Place du Larvotto. The concert was wonderful, and the students looked great in their white formals and black tuxes. There was a Bösendorfer concert grand piano at the site; these pianos were used throughout Europe at our concerts, and they are magnificent. There was quite a crowd for our outdoor concert, and all went well. The mayor of Monaco gave us a post-concert reception. Gifts were exchanged, and the mayor presented me with the flag of Monaco.

Later Connie, Hula Duke, Jean Smoot and I walked down to the Hotel de Paris and the Casino. Crowds gather to watch the Rolls Royces and the heavily be-jeweled women and their escorts as they arrive at these famous places. We had a late supper across the street at a sidewalk café. We walked into the Casino, but didn't dare do any gambling.

We were up at 5:30 a.m. the next morning to start the trip to Zurich. It was rainy, but the sights were interesting – the terraced hills of Italy and the countless tunnels. It was like a toy train set when we

The costumed performers at a show in Innsbruck.

looked at the road below us. We went by Lake Como –made famous by Hemingway's Farewell to Arms – and St. Bernardino, where the St. Bernard dogs are from. Our driver, Paul, wanted us to see a small church at St. Martin, Switzerland, off the highway a small distance. The church was Romanesque, built in 831 and redone in the 1500s. The ceiling was covered with 153 square paintings that you look at with mirrors that are stacked on a table in the center of the church. The kids wanted to sing, so we gave a mini-concert to the visitors in the church.

Zurich is beautiful. We arrived in late evening and found our hotel, the Limmethaus. Switzerland is a training area for hotel management, and it was apparent in our stay there, where we had excellent service.

On Sunday, on our way to Innsbruck for a 4 p.m. concert, the students held a worship service on the bus. They had planned it without my knowing it. We had a scripture reading, prayers, and an anthem. It was a beautiful. The trip through the Alps was breathtaking. We were up where the snow was, with small villages, waterfalls, and avalanche tunnels.

We stopped in Lichtenstein, where the students gave an impromptu concert at the castle where the Duke resides high above the town; there are flowers everywhere. After passing through numerous skiing villages we arrived in Tyrol with its waterfalls, villages with a single spire towering above, and glaciers moving down one meter a year. The lakes are very blue due to the minerals brought down by glaciers.

The concert at Innsbruck, at the Golden Roof, went well, and the crowd was generous with its applause. Caroline Keller was a wonderful emcee and introduced the a cappella program. We visited the Hoflburg Church and the students got permission to sing; they performed Mendelssohn "Heilig" and Nystedt's "I will Praise Thee, O Lord." I was pleased that they loved their music and wanted to share it. We went to a program that night where Tyrolean singers and dancers performed a sort of songfest. We were packed into a large hall, and there was a spirit of fun everywhere.

After a short stay in Salzburg, we arrived in Vienna and got settled in our hotel. The rehearsals for the choral part of the Beethoven Symphony No. 9 were held in the Sofensalle. The chorus to perform at the Danube Centre for the United Nations consisted of a Norwegian girls' chorus, two choirs from Chicago, a Michigan choir, and us. The orchestra was a German youth orchestra that was fabulous. Dr. Denis de Contreau of San Francisco, was the conductor. After a long rehearsal we took the students to the Prater, an amusement park that has the world's largest Ferris wheel. That night we spent a marvelous evening in the Stadtpark, hearing Strauss waltzes and watching the dancers. This is Vienna!

The next morning we attended the rehearsal at the United Nations Plaza. An international festival was in progress, and we saw people from all over the world in native costumes,

Our big concert was held in St. Stephan's Cathedral. I had been in the cathedral in 1974 and was in awe of its beauty. When I was told that we would give a concert there, I was overjoyed as it was one of my ambitions to do so. The concert went well, and I will always treasure the experience to sing in that beautiful cathedral.

The ceremonies at the United Nations Plaza took place the next day. I got to sit with the choirs by wearing the same outfit they had on, otherwise I would not have been allowed to even be in the audience. The nations of the world sent representatives – some were ambassadors, princes, queens, secretaries of state, etc. A wind ensemble from the Vienna Philharmonic played an opening fanfare, and the mayor of Vienna gave the welcoming address. After more speeches and much ceremony, the choirs and orchestra presented the Fourth Movement of Beethoven's Symphony No. 9.

Afterward, the choir presented a concert on a bandstand erected in front of the United Nations Centre that included a special medley of Stephen Foster selections that had been written for us by Robert Page. We did this medley on many occasions on this tour. The program was broadcast throughout Europe. After we had completed the activities at the United Nations Centre the students celebrated with a late meal at a Vienna McDonald's!

The next concert was held at the Wiener Neustadt Cathedral, south of Vienna. The chorus had never sung better or more sensitively. It was as though they were transformed by the 700-year-old cathedral. Bishop Florian and a friend took us all to dinner; they rode on their bicycles to lead the way. The bishop presented me with a large photograph of him taken with the Pope; he was very proud of it and gave it to me as a parting gift. Denny Keller assembled the chorus and had them sing "Heilig" with the words, "danke, auf Wiedersehn." We traveled on to Baden where Beethoven and his nephew came for the baths, and toured the hunting lodge at Meyerling on the way. It was hard to leave beautiful Austria, but we had to go on to Brussels. Once again, the young people led a beautiful worship service while traveling through Austria.

The next concert was at Schloss Rosenau. Built in 1194 but changed over the years until the 1700s, it is now a hotel and a Free Masonry Museum. We sang in a small recital hall to a small audience who stood and sang with us when we did the Austrian national anthem. After lunch in the dining room and a visit to the museum, we continued our journey. At the German border, while we were waiting to be let in, Denny Keller led the group in a political discussion; a marvelous teacher, he led us in many discussions.

We arrived in Nuremburg around five on a Sunday evening. Connie and I had a room at the Hotel Monopol with a large bathroom and a tub! Our hotel owner was a bit wary. Other American groups had stayed there, and she was not looking forward to our stay. However, we quickly changed her outlook. Hula Duke asked her to help find the Lord Mayor so we could give him our Kentucky gifts – tobacco seed, a book on Kentucky, and our finest bourbon.

After relaxing for a while, we headed for Frauenkirche, for our next concert. It went well, and the people were wonderfully receptive, especially an adorable little old lady on the front row. She grabbed Jane Brown's hand and shook it excitedly! We then went to a quaint restaurant, where the owner, Charles Sacher, was wonderful, fluttering around trying everything to please us and make us feel welcome. He certainly succeeded! Some of the group stayed downstairs, but we were seated upstairs and had a marvelous time. The wine flowed, the compliments flowed, and the music flowed. A small group entertained us with Bavarian melodies. A young man played the harp beautifully. The Lord Mayor couldn't come, but a young, handsome chancellor arrived to accept Hula's Kentucky gifts. He stayed with us the rest of the evening. Our hotel owner arrived as well.

At breakfast we had the surprise of the trip – the kids fixed breakfast! The cook did not show up, so we helped the owner out! We had our first breakfast that involved more than a hard bun and coffee. We had meat, cheese, hard-boiled eggs, and juice. Unbelievable!

When we finally loaded up on the bus the hotel owner didn't want us to leave. She stayed and stayed with us on the bus before it pulled out and told us that we were the nicest group she had had there in two and a half years. She kept waving and blowing kisses as we drove off. She was a beautiful girl with long red hair that matched the color of her Irish sweater!

Our experience in Brussels was a world away from our sojourn in Vienna, turning from the ridiculous to the sublime to the horrifying. Our lodgings were a fiasco. They had placed boys and girls in a horrible, smelly annex across from our hotel. I demanded another hotel. As it turned out, the girls were moved back to our hotel, and Paul, our driver, and Louis, our guide from Intropa, moved into the annex with the boys.

After breakfast we went to town to find Jameson Denny, the head of the Kentucky International Tourism Bureau. After finding him we went to a modern church where the kids sang and on to the building that was built for the World's Fair in 1958. Connie and I had lunch at Chez Leon and were just returning from the famous lace shop, Maria Louix, when we saw the police cars and fire trucks. A bomb had exploded near the stage in the Grand' Place where a British Army band was preparing to perform. We looked frantically for our group. The choir was scheduled to perform a half hour later in another square just a block away. We had scheduled the students to meet in the Grand' Place as it was close to where we would perform. I was frantic to get in the cordoned-off area to find my students. I finally got a pass to go through and found them just winding down from being hysterical. Elizabeth Browning fainted and then went into shock, so an ambulance took her to the hospital. The kids were quite upset. We all went to the Place de la Monnaie, where our concert had been scheduled as part of the 1000th anniversary of the founding of Brussels. I decided not to have the concert at this time, and the girl who had organized the concerts for the millennium celebration drove Connie and me to the hospital.

There we saw and talked with members of the British band. Elizabeth was better and was interviewed by a detective from Scotland Yard. After retuning to our hotel we had calls from the American Embassy, the State Department, and the Kentucky Tourism office.

That night Louis, Connie, Hula, Jean and I took a cab to the Grand' Place and ate at a sidewalk café. The Grand' Place is one of the marvels of Western Europe. The proud houses that form the square are memories of an era gone by. There were houses for the masons, sculptors, brewers, painters, bakers, cabinet-makers, and coopers. The buildings, gilded in gold, are illuminated at night. I was glad that we had a chance to sit down and view the beauty of that place after all the excitement and hysteria of the day. This last leg of the trip had worn us all out, and we were ready to go home. But we had two more concerts to do.

We gave our concert at the Place de la Monnaie. Percy Browning stayed at the hospital with her daughter Elizabeth, and I played the accompaniment. The choir did well, but we found out later that another bomb had been discovered just a few feet away from where we were singing. We were advised to leave Brussels and go to Bruges. We spent the afternoon in that lovely town and then returned to Brussels to pack and get ready for our departure.

The Associated Press gave this account of the incident in Brussels:

> "In another blow of a widening IRA terror war, a bomb tore through an open-air stage where a British Army band was preparing to give a concert for tourists. Eleven spectators and four bandsmen were injured. Mayor Pierre von Halteren said the Irish Republican Army claimed responsibility for the bombing – the band that came to Brussels was the Duke of Edinburg's Regiment band, stationed in Ossendorf, West Germany. By chance only six of the 24 members of the band were on stage when the bomb ripped the floor about 3 p.m. The men had stepped off to change into their red dress uniforms after setting up music stands and instruments. The temporary stage had been used for daily concerts to mark Brussels's 1000th birthday this year. A police spokesman said the explosives were under

the stage floor in the back, on the side away from the square."

When we arrived in Cincinnati, we were met by reporters for the Cincinnati Enquirer who wrote, "Mrs. Runyon reported that all instruments were ruined: 'I saw tubas just smashed. Only three choir activities had to be cancelled: a meeting with the mayor, a concert on the splintered stage, and an informal singing event Wednesday. Overall the trip was perhaps the greatest journey a teacher could make with her students in terms of learning about the rest of the world.'"

But after a seven-country whirlwind tour and a front row seat at a terrorist attack, the choir was glad to be home.

Members of the choir were sopranos Elizabeth Browning, Pam Craft, Marla Hatton, Caroline Keller, Maureen McClanahan, Mary Miller, Lu Anne Powell, Judy Robinson, Mary Robinson, Renita Rosser, Ella Williams; altos Sue Arthur, Jayne Brown, Tami Crawford, Diana Heim, Suzanne Hinton, Sarah Richey, Lynea Rosser, Joan Sapp, Karen Silvey, Becky Tollner, Sheila Wilson; tenors Philip Grigson, Mark Hester, Doug McClananan, Doug Powell, Robert Roe, Jimmy Rosser, Dennison Keller, Jr.; basses Richard Blake, Robbie Bowkamp, Peter Browning, Kent Kalb, Jeff Lytle, Robert McHugh, Bill Phillips, Chuck Preston, James Rice, Karen Silvey, Ray Sparks, John Waldren. Chaperones were Lillian Crawford, Mary Louise Duke, Connie Ford, Eula Fowler, Donna Hatton, Alvina Henson, Carolanne Keller, R. Dennison Keller, Anne Parker, Betty Phillips, Bertha Preston, Helen Robinson, Russell Robinson, Sue Rosser, Jean Smoot.

After the second trip to Vienna, the following concerts represent the musical depth of the singers. In the spring concert of May 1, 1980, my son Randy was the accompanist.

The program follows:

Mass in Time of War	Haydn

　　Judy Robinson, soprano; Renita Rosser, soprano; Cathy Phillips, alto; Becky Tollner, alto; Richard Blake, tenor; Kent Kalb, bass

　　The Concert Choir

Ave Maria	Verdi
The Falcon	Gerrish

How Lovely Is Thy Dwelling Place	Brahms
The Concert Choir	
Piping Down the Valleys	Korte
Sebben Crudele	Caldara
Judy Robinson	
Come, Let Us Start a Joyful Song	Hassler
The Girls' Ensemble	
Go, Lovely Rose	Thiman
The Girls' Chorus	
O Sing Unto the Lord	Dello Joio
Climbin' Up the Mountain	arr. Smith
The Boys' Ensemble	
Hop Up My Ladies	arr. Gilbert
Robert Roe, Kent Kalb, Richard Blake, James Rice	
Der Neugierige	Schubert
Kent Kalb	
Stopping By Woods on a Snowy Evening	Thompson
The Boys' Glee Club	
Suite pour le piano	Debussy
Richard Blake, piano	
Allegro, from Concerto in G Minor	Vivaldi
Cathy Phillips, violin	
I Attempt from Love's Sickness to Fly	Purcell
The Vagabond	Vaughan Williams
Mein	Schubert
Richard Blake, baritone	
One of Those Songs	Calvi
Roll, Jordan, Roll	arr. Gillum
O Bella Fusa	di Lasso
The Mixed Ensemble	
In These Delightful Pleasant Groves	Purcell
The Madrigal Singers	
Every Time I Feel the Spirit	arr. Dawson
Great Day	Youmans
The Concert Choir	

For the Christmas Concert on December 14, 1980, Brian Patton, who was doing his student teaching with me, was the accompanist. The Concert Choir presented the following program:

Gott, der Herr, ist Sonn' und Schild	Bach
Veni Jesu	Cherubini
How Lovely Are the Messengers	Mendelssohn
Awake the Harp	Haydn
Heilig (for double choir)	Mendelssohn
Blow, Blow, Thou Winter Wind	Rutter
Ave Maria	Rachmaninoff
Psalm 100 (for double choir)	Schutz
Saul	Hovland

    Jim Rannes, narrator

Selections from "Messiah"   Handel
    Overture, Recitative: Comfort Ye, Air: Every Valley
    Michael Bolden, tenor; Chorus: And the Glory; Chorus: For Unto Us a Child Is Born; Chorus: Hallelujah!

For the May 17, 1981, Spring Concert, Brian Patton was the accompanist and the program was:

Tu Es Petrus	Palestrina
Surely He Hath Borne Our Griefs	Graun
Libera me, from Requiem	Fauré

    James Rice, Chris Scott, Ron Kimble, Bill Phillips, and Keith Bolden, baritone soloists

Jubilate Deo	Peeters
How Excellent Thy Name	Hanson
O del dolce mio ardor	Gluck

    Mary Robinson, soprano

Shepherds, Would Ye Hope to Please Us   Rowley
    The Girls' Ensemble

Vergebliches Standchen   Brahms
    Renita Rosser, soprano

O Pastorelle, Addio   Giordano
    The Girls' Chorus

Intermezzo, Op. 18, No. 2   Brahms

Brian Patton, piano	
Song of Peace	Persichetti
Do You Fear the Wind	Sateren
The Boys' Ensemble	
Gia il sole dal Gange	Scarlatti
Tim Hiles, bass	
Down in the Valley	Mead
The Boys' Glee Club	
Neighbors' Chorus	Offenbach
All My Trials	arr. Luboff
Renita Rosser, soprano	
Shoot False Love, I Care Not	Morley
The Madrigal Singers	
Hava Nageela	arr. Goldman
I'm Gonna Sing	Junter
The Man of La Mancha	Leigh

For a number of years at the Morehead State University music festival, a student would be selected as the outstanding vocalist of the day. This was sponsored by the Kentucky Music Teachers' Association, a part of the National Association of Music Teachers. Each year one of my students would be selected, and we would go to the next level, which was to compete in a state contest with the winners from the different regions. Many times after winning the state contest, the student would not be able to attend the national finals. In 1979 my student Richard Blake was chosen at Morehead. We prepared the required three pieces, and he won the state contest.

The finals were in Seattle. I was not able to go with Richard and his mother who made the trip; he came in second in the finals. The next year, Richard was again chosen at Morehead, won the state contest, and won the Southern Division Contest in Deland, Florida. I was determined that I would attend the finals, to be held in Washington, D. C. He won the national contest! I have had a lot of thrills in my teaching career, but this surely ranks at the top! He performed on a program with the National Symphony Orchestra along with the winning violinist and college piano winner.

Richard, after graduating from high school and college, entered medical school, and is now a heart specialist in Lexington, Kentucky. His father Robert Blake, another physician, has been a piano student of mine for several years. In the past year I told "Dr. Bob" that he should work up a "recital." I gave a dinner party, and he was the featured performer. One of the guests was my violin pupil of 1941, Richard Zeigler, and he and Bob performed harmonica duets after the piano recital!

In 1981 I had a visiting delegation from the Department of Education in Frankfort. They observed my teaching in the Straub Elementary School on a day I was teaching a small group of beginning violin students. A few days later, I was surprised with another group of visitors who accompanied Superintendent Felice Felice to my room to announce that I had been selected Kentucky's Teacher of the Year for 1982. I was very proud and extremely honored. It was a long way from Orangeburg.

I resigned at the end of the school year in the spring of 1982 but continued my teaching at Maysville Community College. It was a very hard decision to make, but I had married Earle D. Jones and he pointed out that I had given many years to teaching and deserved a rest. I retired from teaching at the Mason County Schools, supremely grateful for the many joys I had there. All my superintendents – Hubert Hume, Charles Straub, and Felice Felice – were wonderful to me. I loved running to the county schools and teaching the junior high students – always looking for the especially talented ones. I found so many students with an intense love for music – so many students with outstanding voices, just waiting to be taught!

Chapter 11:
Music at Maysville Community College
"Higher Education"

In April 1968, Dr. Charles Wethington, president of the newly formed Maysville Community College, called me and offered me the position of music instructor. M. Glynn Burke, who had been pastor at the First Christian Church when I was music director there, had written a letter on my behalf. It said, in part:

> "I write in reference to and recommendation of Mrs. Harold (Coralie) Runyon who, I understand, is being considered as a professor in music at the college... Mrs. Runyon is one of the most capable vocal music teachers I have ever known – including my present experience in this University and College town. She has unusual gifts in her field – not only in the knowledge and skill with music but likewise with people. And with this tremendous ability – I am honestly inclined to say genius – she combines the will to work, a personal discipline, and a determination for excellence!
>
> In addition to her unusual competence and cooperation, Mrs. Runyon is a person with keen insight, profound thoughts and broad culture... As director of our music program and adult choir she attracted many people into the church by the quality of her own personality as well as the obvious quality of her music leadership.
>
> If this seems over enthusiastic it is no less a realistic and honest appraisal and merely reflects my sincere high regard for Coralie Runyon. I am sure she would be a great asset to the college."

I began teaching at the college on August 28, 1968. Classes were held in the Trinity Methodist Church and the First Presbyterian Church downtown. I taught music theory and the college choir. There were 14 members in this first chorus for the college, and I named it the Chamber Singers.

The first concert was held December 13, 1968, in the First Presbyterian Church's first-floor assembly room. The accompanist was Kathy Wright, a talented member of my high school chorus and the accompanist for the England choir trip the previous summer.

Here is the program:

I:	For Us A Child Is Born	Bach
	Michaelynn Wallingford, soprano; Gary Patrick Biddle, tenor; William Wheat, baritone	
II:	Cantique of Jean Racine	Fauré
III:	Lay Down Your Staffs, O Shepherds	Old French
	Bring a Torch Jeannette, Isabella	arr. Shaw
	The Holy Infant's Lullabye	Dello Joio
	Genrose Turner, soprano	
	A Babe Is Born	Moe
IV:	Jubilate Deo	Cooper
	The Shepherds' Chorus	Menotti
	Song of Praise	Sitton

Members were: Nancy Combs, June Kilgus, Ann Thompson, Genrose Turner, sopranos; Mary Milton Anderson, Zoe Chamness, Michaelynn Wallingford, Betty Wood, altos; Gary Biddle, David Grigson, Mike Marinaro, tenors; Lowell Cooper, James Heller, William Wheat, basses

Dr. Hugh Henderson, dean of fine arts at the University of Kentucky, was in the audience and was amazed at the quality of music performed by a community college choir. He wrote Dr. Wethington and invited the choir to perform on the university campus. We did so on June 18, 1969. The concert was held in the Agricultural Science Auditorium, and I was surprised to see all members of the music faculty in attendance. In a receiving line after the concert, one of the music faculty members shook my hand and said, "We were sent a memo that we must attend this concert. I wondered why. Now I know."

The choir had now grown to 18 members and we gave this program:

I:	Missa Brevis	Mozart
	Genrose Turner, Nancy Combs, sopranos;	

        Michaelynne Wallingford, contralto; David Grigson, Michael Marinaro, tenors; William Wheat, baritone

II: Six Chansons   Hindemith
III: Blow the Candles Out   arr. Smith
     Pretty Mary   Thompson
     Devilish Mary   Thompson

    The Chamber Singers: Nancy Combs, Patti Hord, Connie Runyon, Ann Thompson, Genrose Turner, sopranos; Nancy Hanson, Michaelynn Wallingford, Betty Wood, altos; Ricky Alexander, David Grigson, Michael Marinaro, Winn Turner, tenors; Lowell Cooper, Robert Jones, Dan Kemplin, William Wheat, basses.

    The choir continued to grow and the 22-member Chamber Singers gave a concert in December 1969 in the new college auditorium. The program featured two major works: The "Magnificat" by Antonio Vivaldi and the "Christmas Cantata" by Daniel Pinkham. Soloists in the Magnificat were Sue Cropper, Genrose Turner, Mary Milton Anderson, and Ricky Alexander. U.K. provided a chamber orchestra and a double brass choir to accompany these two works.

The College Choir performing at graduation services held on the lawn in the early '70s.

The Chamber Singers were composed of Priscilla Browning, Linda Case, Sue Cropper, Ann Hardymon, Ann Thompson, Genrose Turner, sopranos; Mary Milton Anderson, Cathy Curtis, Nancy Hanson, Carla Osborne, Connie Robinson, altos; Ricky Alexander, Norman Allen, Steve Mallory, Phil Marinaro, Michael Marinaro, Phillip Sledd, tenors; Lowell Cooper, George Day, Henry Jefferson, Jr., William Wheat, Jerry Zeigler, basses.

As the choir continued to grow, I changed the name to the Concert Choir of Maysville Community College. I continued to program major works, and the choristers delighted in performing music of this depth. Some of these were: Neue Liebeslieder, Op. 65, Brahms; Missa Sancti Nicholas, Haydn; Te Deum, Mozart; Magnificat, Vivaldi; Mass in G, Schubert; the Wedding Cantata, Pinkham; Ceremony of Carols, Britten; Te Deum, Haydn; Magnificat in C, Pachelbel; Rejoice in the Lamb, Britten; Requiem, Brahms; Messiah, Handel; Solemn Mass, Vierne; Psalmkomzert, Zimmerman; Selections from Vesperae solemnes de confessore, Mozart; Song of the Open Road, Dello Joio; Gloria, Poulenc; Requiem, Fauré; Requiem, Rutter; Arise, Your Light Has Come, Danner; For Us a Child Is Born, Bach; Christmas Day, Holst; Te Deum, Rutter; Hodie, VaughanWilliams; Gloria, Rutter; Missa Brevis, Willan; Fantasia on Christmas Carols, Vaughan Williams. Lighter works included "A Montage of Songs of George Gershwin," arr. Ades; "A Montage of Songs of Rodgers and Hammerstein," arr. Jay Flippin; "A Sentimental Jouney through the Forties," arr. Ades; "A Century of Song: Irvin Berlin and Jerome Kern," "A Choral Portrait," Hayward; "The Phantom of the Opera," Webber.

In December 1971, the college choir and the Mason County High School Choir combined to present Handel's "Messiah." The soloists for this work were Robert Myers, one of my former students and now a freshman at Morehead State University, tenor; Kenton Cooper, counter-tenor; Anne Beane, soprano; and James Ross Beane, baritone. The program was held at the First Christian Church with James Clarke, organist, on the new Holloway pipe organ.

This interesting editorial appeared in the Daily Independent on May 3, 1972:

Community College Changing Ideals

Among the happiest aspects that the Maysville Community College has brought to us is an accelerated interest in music. Not that our town and area were ever lacking in rich musical opportunities since our Maysville Schools have won deserved fame under their soon-to-be-gone director, Dr. John K. Farris, and the same good fortune has prevailed with our choral music in public and private schools. It is true too in our churches. But good as the music is, it cannot compare with the enrichment offered through facilities of the Community College, be they symphonic, choral, strings, ballet, piano. Every stratum of our society and all ages now may be exposed to beautiful music, and as John Ruskin once said, it is by listening that the ear can be cultivated to a higher taste in music. Far more is accomplished, however, than the opportunity for society to broaden its taste and widen its horizons. For example, there is the Maysville Community College Concert Choir, which will give two major choral works at it annual spring concert Tuesday night. The Bach work will be accompanied by a chamber orchestra and Tirro's American Jazz Mass will be accompanied by a jazz combo.

What this signifies is that the College now offers young people and adults opportunities to develop their own musical gifts. The members are those of the Concert Choir and Limestone Youth Orchestra.

The cultural impact of the Community college is inestimable. It makes available also our Fine Arts Series. To mention these is not to minimize the advantages afforded through our two-year college program, combining basic learning tools with technical skills such as in business or the new nursing project soon to start....

The significance of the Maysville Community College is that it shall become a balancing wheel between the material and the cultural. For a long time people have been saying that civilization has lost its soul and certainly its classical tradition.

We cannot expect within a single generation for a junior

college to exert sufficient influence to meet the needs essential to modern man. Our definition of essentiality in this sense is that there is a desperate need in our world for men of spacious, ample minds equipped to meet real problems and to keep alive great patterns of social behavior.

Nonetheless, the College can generate new ideals. This it is doing. One of them is to create a listening ear. As man becomes more aware of the harmony in music, he inevitably becomes more attuned to the music of the universe. In acquiring both disciplines, he can but lose some of his restlessness, thereby dissipating his apparent urge for constant motion, spending, and an unending search for pleasure..."

The College Choir presented this concert in the college auditorium. Bach's "Christ Lag in Todesbanden" was accompanied by a chamber orchestra composed of Karen Jones, Melissa Smoot, Dorothy Browning, C. J. Hunter, Melissa Turner, violins; Elizabeth Smart and Toy Stewart, violas; John K. Farris, cello; Marla Kalb, piano. The American Jazz Mass by Frank P. Tirro was accompanied by a jazz combo with Norman Yeager, trumpet; Steve Jones, alto saxophone, John K. Farris, baritone saxophone, Elizabeth Smart, string bass, and Paul Hunt, percussion. The choir members included Sherry Barbee, Priscilla Browning, Christy Clark, Mary V. Clarke, Nancy Combs, Kathy Kreidler, Nancy Osborne, Peggy Rigdon, Melissa Turner, Michelene Brannen, Ginny Browning, Charlene Cracraft, Sally Greifenkamp, Maria Harrison, Elizabeth Smart, Laura Sparks, Carol Trumbo, James L. Clarke, Lowell D. Cooper, Bill Harrison, Dale Phelps, John C. Scott, Jeffrey Worthington, Thomas Baxter, John C. Calvert, Charles Calvert, John R. Denham, Paul Hunt, Frederick Roberts, Jr., Tim Teegarden, and Lynn Todd.

In the fall of 1972 the music department of Indiana University at Bloomington contacted me and asked if they could present Menotti's "Amahl and the Night Visitors" in Maysville. The concert was arranged, and I trained the chorus and organized the orchestra for the concert on November 20, 1972. I asked James Beane to conduct the orchestra, and I enjoyed playing in it. The concert was held in the Opera Theater and had the support of the Community College, the Kentucky Arts

Commission and the National Endowment for the Arts.

It was a great feeling of satisfaction that so many of the young string players had become advanced enough to accompany choral groups at the college and at the high school. The Limestone Youth Orchestra was in full swing, and many of its members were playing exceedingly well. Small groups were formed and many performances were given in churches, and for Frontier Christmas celebrations in Old Washington. Several of the students were accepted for All-State Orchestra, and some have gone on to make a profession of playing a stringed instrument.

The Chamber Singers presented an outstanding concert on April 30, 1973, programming three major works. The first was Schubert's Mass in G with Nancy Osborn, Melissa Turner and Betty Fraley singing the soprano solos; Phil Marinaro the tenor solos, and Robert Blake and Christopher Browning the bass solos. Accompaniment was provided by the Limestone String Quartet, composed of Karen Jones and Sharon Thomas, violins, Elizabeth Smart, viola, and Elaine Hansen, cello. The "Wedding Cantata" by Pinkham followed with solos by Judy Kennan and Phil Marinaro. Judy Kennan presented a group of soprano solos: "Alleluia" by Mozart, "O Mio Babbino Caro" by Puccini, "Deh Vieni" by Mozart, and "Mon coeur s'ouvre à ta voix" by Saint-Saens. I had taught Judy since she was in the 8th grade. I would have her to come to the high school in the afternoon after school and "sit on the stool" to listen while I was teaching the high school students vocal solos. When I felt she was read to start studying voice, we began when she was in high school. She was later involved in a car accident and faced many challenges but continued her vocal training and did some professional work in Florida.

The last number on the concert was the "Psalmconzert" by Zimmerman and featured a brass ensemble accompaniment and a Children's Choir.

On Dec. 7, 1973, the Chamber Singers presented a concert in the college auditorium that included Mozart's Te Deum, "Three Motets for the Season of Christmas" by Poulenc, and Vivaldi's Magnificat, accompanied by a chamber orchestra. The concluding group of numbers comprised "A Boy Was Born" by Britten, "I Wonder as I Wander" by Niles, Mozart's Laudate Dominum, and "Silent Night" arranged by

chapter eleven

Norman Luboff.

I resigned from the college in 1973 but continued teaching in the Mason County Schools and working with the Limestone Youth Orchestra.

In 1985, Dr. Harry Benson, interim president of the college, called and asked me to return to the college. In 1979 I had married Earle D. Jones, and he was supportive of my returning to teaching at the college. I taught classes in the humanities, and enjoyed them thoroughly. I also developed a new college choir and was overjoyed when the Hayswood Foundation presented me with a concert grand piano to use. This was the second grand piano that I had received – the first was given to me by the Browning Foundation to use at Mason County High School.

The new choir of approximately 70 members was a fine group. In its first year we presented five concerts that were exceedingly well received.

The College Choir gave a special performance on March 24, 1985, for the Maysville Community College Board of Advocates. Dr. Hubert Henderson, dean of the College of Fine Arts of the University of Kentucky, was in the audience and was impressed with the quality of music. He invited us to perform on the Sunday Series at the university's

With Gov. Martha Layne Collins.

Center for the Arts. The College Choir performed at Trinity Methodist Church for the Community Good Friday Service on April 5, singing "O Vos Omnes" by Casals. On April 21 the choir gave a concert at the First Presbyterian Church. James L. Clarke, our accompanist, shared the program with the choir, presenting several organ selections.

Martha Comer wrote the following account of the program in her "Do You Know" column in the Ledger-Independent:

"The concert Sunday by the Maysville Community College Choir brought tears to my eyes, caused me to pray and to be filled with such pride that there were friends and neighbors making music that would be a credit to the Cincinnati Symphony. From the moment that Jim Clarke played the Bach fugue I knew that would be a special afternoon. It was great that he added a sprightly Handel piece to remind us that this is the anniversary of these two masters. But Jim at the organ was just a wonderful beginning to this holy of holy afternoons. Coralie Jones had made superb choices for a concert to be given in the beautiful First Presbyterian Church.... Peace filled my heart as it did others in the crowded sanctuary. As people arrived, they sat comfortably in their seats, I heard comments such as these: 'Well, anything that Coralie and Jim Clarke do is bound to be excellent.' It is my greatest musical pleasure to hear them. And apparently there are others who think so, too."

On April 24 the Choir gave a program at the Maysville County Club. On December 8, the College Choir sang at a vesper service in the Old Church Museum for Frontier Christmas in Washington. An article in the Ledger-Independent the following day stated, "The special reason for this year's success was the music presented by the Maysville Community College Choir. The congregation was held in holy silence as the 60 voices were lifted in song to honor the Savior. Unforgettable was the singing of 'Silent Night for which Raleigh Kincaid, music director of Trinity Methodist Church, was the soloist."

We presented a concert in the recital hall of the University of Kentucky on November 10, 1985. Numbers included "Vere Languores" by Victoria, "Laudate Dominum" by Mozart, "Libera Me" from Fauré's

"Requiem," the "Hallelujah" from "The Mount of Olives" by Beethoven, Poulenc's "Gloria," "All My Trials," a Bahamian Spiritual, "Ain't-a That Good News," arranged by Dawson; and "Glorious Everlasting" by Cousins.

On December 19 the Choir presented Handel's "Messiah" at the First Presbyterian Church.

The year 1986 was also busy for the Maysville Community College Choir. We presented a program for the Mason County Homemakers annual meeting with "A Salute to Broadway." The spring concert was held in the Maysville High School Auditorium and the program featured Fauré's "Requiem," Brahms's "Liebeslieder Waltzes," selections from Mozart's "Vesperae solemnes de Confessore" and selections from Rodgers and Hammerstein. James L. Clarke was the accompanist and he was joined by John W. McNeill in a duet accompaniment for the Brahms number.

The College Choir was again invited to appear on the Sunday Series in the U.K. Center for the Arts. This time the performance was held in the concert hall and included Haydn's "Te Deum," John Rutter's "Gloria," Norman Luboff's arrangement of "All My Trials" and "Deep River," and Smith's arrangement of "Plenty Good Room." The program concluded with "A Montage of Songs of George Gershwin," arranged by Ades and "A Montage of Songs of Rodgers and Hammerstein," arranged by Jay Flippin. Jay is an outstanding musician, an excellent educator and fine jazz pianist who has taught at Morehead for many years. We have worked together many times and I always enjoy his talent.

Earle Jones was proud of the choir and the work I was doing with them and he sent a special invitation to all of his friends – many of whom were former basketball coaches, as he had been. I was amazed to see many of these men seated in a long row together.

The Christmas concert was held in the First Presbyterian Church on December 21. The program opened with the Sweelinck "Hodie Christus Natus Est" and was followed by Haydn's "Te Deum," "The Shepherd's Story" by Dickinson, "The Shepherds' Farewell" by Berlioz, and Kuykendall's arrangement of "Joy to the World." The audience joined in a group of familiar carols and Rutter's "Gloria" concluded the program.

The College Choir received an invitation to sing at the annual Governor's Derby Breakfast at the State Capitol on May 2, 1987. We gave two programs there; one in the morning at the Governor's Mansion, and the other in the afternoon in front of the capitol annex. The programs consisted of a tribute to the music of Stephen Foster and George Gershwin as well as a group of spirituals. The members of the choir were guests at the Derby brunch. It was an exciting day and Governor Martha Layne Collins was most gracious to us.

On November 1, the College Choir presented a concert at the Episcopal Church of the Nativity. Martha Comer wrote in the Ledger-Independent:

> "The saints are credited with having said, "Singing is twice praying," and this was reaffirmed Sunday as the Maysville Community College Choir shared with the congregation a program of "singing prayerfully." Gabriel Fauré's magnificent and deeply spiritual "Requiem" was presented at the Episcopal Church of the Nativity, with the choir singing in Latin as the people followed the translation in English. "It was absolutely a tremendous experience," was the summation of the capacity crowd filling the old church for another of its programs marking the 150th anniversary of the parish founding. If there was any part of the "Mass" more poignant than others, it was the "Libera Me" (Deliver me from death's everlasting fire on the Day of Judgment) as sung by Scott Poe, baritone. Claiming no less distinction was Robin Sutherland's singing of the "Pie Jesu" (Blessed Lord Jesus, I pray in thy mercy grant them rest, grant them everlasting rest). But without exception, all in the church and especially the choristers found the singing of "Agnus Dei" (Lamb of God) to be an act of holy spirituality."

The Christmas Concert was given on December 20 at the Church of the Nativity and was highlighted by "Hodie" by Ralph Vaughan Williams. After an intermission we sang "Blow, Blow, Thou Winter Wind" by Rutter, "Laudate Dominum" by Mozart, "The Little Drummer Boy," arranged by McCarthy, and "The Christmas Song," arranged by Knight.

The College Choir gave a spring concert April 23, 1989, in the

chapter eleven

Mason County High School choral room: "Psalm 100" by Schutz with an antiphonal part for brass choir, "Thou, O Jehovah, Abideth Forever" by Copland, "Cantique of Jean Racine" by Fauré, "O Clap Your Hands" and "A Gaelic Blessing" by Rutter, "Cry Out and Shout" by Nystedt, and "Now is the Month of Maying" by Morley. The second half of the program was the presentation of "A Century of Song" by Irving Berlin.

On December 3, 1989, the College Choir was thrilled to be asked to perform on the Rosemary Clooney Christmas Show held at Music Hall in Cincinnati. The first part of the program consisted of "There Shall A Star From Jacob Come Forth" by Mendelssohn and "Go Tell It on the Mountain" arranged by Rutter, sung by the College Choir. Debbie Boone, daughter of Pat Boone, was featured in "Silent Night" and "Joy to the World," after which the choir returned to sing with Rosemary Clooney "The Old Man," "Snow," "Count Your Blessings" and "White Christmas." These numbers had been sent to me by Rosemary's arranger, John Oddo. He also conducted the orchestra for this part of the program. James L. Clarke accompanied the College Choir in the numbers we sang alone. It was a great thrill to sing in Music Hall and to be in the concert with Rosemary.

Seven days later the college choir presented its Christmas concert at Trinity Methodist Church. The choir processed while singing "Arise, Your Light Has Come" by Danner. This was followed by the Bach cantata, " For Us A Child Is Born." Then followed "Here Is the Little Door" by Howell, "Nativity Carol" by Rutter, "Ding Dong, Merrily On High" by Near, and "Christmas Day" by Holst. Rutter's "Te Deum" concluded the concert.

The 1990 spring concert included "Exultate, Justi" by Viadana, "Laudate Pueri" by Mozart, "Song of the Open Road" by Dello Joio, "Life Is Happiness Indeed" by Bernstein; "Jerome Kern: A Choral Portrait" arranged by Hayward, and selections from Webber's "The Phantom of the Opera." The accompanist for the concert was Suzan Haughaboo.

On December 9, the Ensemble Company of the Cincinnati Opera presented Menotti's opera "Amahl and the Night Visitors" in the Opera House, with the College Choir singing the choral part.

On December 16, the choir presented its Christmas concert in

Trinity United Methodist Church. James L. Clarke was the accompanist and the program featured "Let All Mortal Flesh Keep Silence" by Bairstow (Michael Wallingford, tenor), "The Lord Is My Shepherd" by Rutter, "He, Watching over Israel" by Mendelssohn, "Solemn Mass" by Vierne; Allelua from "Exultate, Jubilate" by Mozart (Catherine Clarke, soprano), "The Jesus Gift" by Martin (Kent Kalb, baritone), "Ding, Dong, Merrily on High" arranged by Willocks, "Candlelight Carol" and "Christmas Lullabye" by Rutter, and "O Holy Night" by Adam, arranged by Rutter.

The College Choir presented "Music and the Spoken World" on December 8, 1991, at the Trinity Methodist church. Dr. Jack Lundy, dean of the college, worked with me in preparing a program on which he read several appropriate selections. The program included "Greet the Dawning" by Sanborn, "Missa Brevis" by Willan, "In the Bleak Mid-Winter" by Darke, "A Babe is Born" by Mathias, "What Sweeter Music" by Rutter, "I Wonder As I Wander" by Niles, "Fantasia on Christmas Carols" by Vaughan Williams, and "Arise, Your Light Has Come" by Danner.

This Christmas concert was the last one I gave with the College Choir. I resigned from the college early in 1991. Earle had suffered a dreadful stroke in 1988 and was not able to speak again. He received excellent care from doctors in Maysville and Lexington, but it was decided that he should be placed in the Maysville Extended Care facility. I was reluctant, but realized that it was for the best. I went to see him every day unless I had to be out of town. I worked constantly with him, hoping that he could speak again and recover from this heart-breaking state of health. All the therapies that were tried, all the tests that were done were to no avail. I resigned from the college to devote all my time to him.

Several years passed. I agreed to organize another singing group. Rehearsals would be at night so that I could stay with Earle during the day. He died in 1998 after suffering another stroke.

Earle D. Jones was a much-loved man. He was a famous basketball coach as well as a principal and superintendent of the Maysville Schools. We had a wonderful time together for nearly nine years before he had the stroke. We spent time each winter in Florida, and traveled a good deal.

chapter eleven

He was interested in my music, my pupils, and my accomplishments. He was an elder in the First Christian Church, as was I, and the church occupied a big place in our lives. We had a host of marvelous friends and we entertained with many dinner parties at his home on Third Street. I have been blessed to have known two wonderful husbands, Harold and Earle.

Chapter 12:
The Limestone Youth Orchestra
"String Music"

Though I focused on choral music for most of my 64 years of teaching, I am thrilled to have been able to start a string program 35 years ago. Since I had been trained as a violinist, I wanted my students to have the opportunity to experience the wonders and joys of orchestra. With the assistance of the University of Kentucky and the Maysville Community College, where I was the music instructor in addition to my work with the Mason County Schools, we began to make a string program a reality. We set up a program to offer free violin lessons to interested fourth grade students in the schools. With Peter Shafer, a member of the U.K. faculty, I visited the elementary schools to explain the program. Plans were made to audition 40 boys and girls for a pilot program with the beginning set for January 15, 1969. Classes were held at the Mason County High School music room. Mr. Shafer, a native of Germany, was educated at the Berlin High School of Music, the Munich Conservatory and the Paris Conservatory. He did further study at the Mannes College of Music, New York, and in l968 he was the assistant conductor of the Philadelphia Orchestra. What an opportunity for our boys and girls! It seems unbelievable that my students had the opportunity to study with such a talented artist.

On September 14, 1960, Rodney Farrar, another U.K. faculty member, gave a program at the Maysville Community College for students interested in learning to play the cello. A graduate of Oberlin College and a cellist with the Rochester, New York, Philharmonic Orchestra, he gave free lessons to students in the fourth, fifth, and sixth grades. Miss Nancy Smith, a junior at U.K., also came to Maysville to teach cello. I was fortunate that I could take lessons from her.

By 1970 I had decided to form an orchestra with the 40 string students. On each Saturday the group met in the student lounge at the community college for rehearsal. One of my eager and dedicated members was Kitty Hunter, the grandmother of one of the fourth graders, C.J. She was an inspiration to me, and she would slip me a

chapter twelve

dollar or so each Saturday morning to buy strings, rosin, and music for the group. C.J. developed into a fine violinist and after I retired in 1982 he became the music director of the Mason County Schools. He has since developed a large string program there in addition to the choral program.

I also sought the help of John K. Farris, the director of instrumental music in the Maysville Schools. Johnny was one of the best band directors I have ever known and a fine string bass player. He came to the Saturday rehearsals, carrying a battered black suitcase with battered music stands as we were without any funds for the necessities of an orchestral program. I named the group the Limestone Youth Orchestra and a board of directors was appointed. They were Mrs. Robert (Percy) Browning, president, Mrs. Robert (Naomi) Blake, vice-president, James L. Clarke, secretary, Earl Linquist, Maysville Community College President Dr. Charles Wethington, Dr. Joseph McKinnery, and me.

The board of directors printed 4,000 copies of a brochure and distributed it to all the schools of the area:

The Maysville-Mason County area is fortunate, indeed, in having an organization such as the Limestone Youth Orchestras. This organization is providing musical training in orchestral music for children of all ages.

One year ago this month, this small group of 40 players held its first rehearsal. Two months later, a four-day music camp was held

A 1970 concert. My daughter Connie is the cellist far right.

for all members providing private instruction, sectional rehearsals, full orchestral rehearsal, elementary theory and recreation, ending with its first real concert in the library of the Maysville Community College. In the fall of 1970, weekly rehearsals were held every Saturday morning at the Community College. At Christmas three concerts were presented at the Orangeburg Elementary School, Washington Elementary School, and the Opera Theater in Maysville. By concert time, the orchestra had grown to 65 members. The spring weekly rehearsals have continued, students are participating in class and private lessons. In February, a musical workshop was held by Mr. Orville Dally, Dayton, Ohio.

The string program now includes two orchestras: a beginning group of over 15 children which meets with Mr. John K. Farris and the senior group with Mrs. Runyon. This summer there will be two music camps – one for advanced students starting on June 7, and one for beginning students on June 14. During July and August there will be practice sessions and ensembles, quartets, trios, and duet-playing three days a week and full orchestra rehearsal once a week...

The Limestone Youth Orchestra is a volunteer group providing instruction, enjoyment, entertainment and musical development for the youth in this area. We need your interest, your children, and your financial support regardless how large or small. With your help this Limestone Youth Orchestra can be continued!

Financial help came, and the orchestra continued to grow and develop. We needed a larger rehearsal room, so we used the band room at the high school and the second orchestra was formed: a beginners' group called the Concert Orchestra. Teachers from Morehead State University came on Saturdays and were available for private lessons after the orchestra rehearsals.

The music camps were wonderful experiences for the orchestra members. They were held at the adjoining homes of Mr. and Mrs. Robert Browning and Mr. and Mrs. L. L. Browning, Jr. A large room on the first level of Percy's home was used for rehearsal, and students could be seen practicing all over the beautiful lawns of both houses after their daily lessons.

The first camp was held in 1970. The faculty was headed by Joseph

chapter twelve

Ceo of U.K., who also was conductor of the Central Youth Symphony Orchestra. Other faculty from Lexington included Miss Nancy Snith, Miss Sue Lamberson, Miss Mary Ogletree, and Clyde Gilpin. John Blackmarr, Jr., from Louisville, Miss Helen Greim, and I completed the list. Supervision in recreation and swimming in the beautiful pool between the two estates was done by Mr. L. L. Browning, Jr., Mrs. Nancy Helton, Miss Theresa Hillenmeyer, Miss Virginia Browning, and Miss Christy Clark.

The first concert of the Limestone Youth Orchestra was presented at the conclusion of the camp in the library of the Maysville Community College. The program follows:

March in G	Purcell
Sinfonia	McKay
Prelude, Dance, Finale	
Scherzo	Webster
Cheryl Beane, Cello	
Three Famous Hymns	arr. Applebaum
Hymn of Praise, With Each New Day, Our Future Hopes	
Suite	Riegger
Minuet, Czardas, Minuet, March of the Hobgoblins On Distant Strands	
Krazy Klock	Ployhar
When Johnny Comes Marching Home	Matesky

Members of the orchestra were: violin I: Karen Jones, C. J. Hunter, Melissa Turner, Joan Johnson; violin II: Katherine Wood, Terry Brown, Mindy Bernardin, Tim Marinaro; violin III: Dan Burton, Linda Turner, Penny Grigson, Debbie McNutt, Michele Bernardin, Sharon Thomas, Tara Boggs, Jeanie Dorn, Betty Fraley, Pam Jefferson, Jackie Jones; violas: Elizabeth Smart, Toy Stewart; cellos: Mary Blakefield, Cheryl Beane, Henry Jefferson, David Gallenstein, Kitty H. Hunter, Keith Browning; bass: Kurt Hook, David Anderson; flute: Marsha Owens, Virginia Johnson; oboe: Pam Leforge; bassoon: Kathy Boone; clarinet: Georgia Osborne, Donna Combs, Leslie Sapp, Linda Coburn, Alice Stewart; alto saxophone: Elaine Hansen; French horn: Robbie Blake, Billy Bean, Nancy Combs; trumpet: Stockton Wood,

Timmy Hensen, Terry Throroughman; trombone: David Blake, Andy Combs; percussion: Paul Hunt.

In 1971, violinist Mrs. Ronald Haun came to Maysville. Her husband was the principal of the Orangeburg School, and they were a welcome addition to the music and educational scene. Mrs. Haun gave private violin lessons and presented a recital of her pupils on December 15, 1971 at the Maysville Community College.

The Limestone Youth Orchestra performed on June 11, 1971, at the Washington Methodist Church Museum prior to the second music camp. The string orchestra played "Theme and Variations" by Green, "Viola Caprice" by Muller (Elizabeth Smart, viola), and "Sinfonia" by Stamitz-Green. The Limestone Youth Orchestra performed "Now Let Every Tongue Adore Thee" by Bach, "Allegro" by Clementi," and "Sarabande and Allegro" by Clementi-Muller. Teachers assisting in the instruction were Joseph Ceo, John K. Farris, and Connie Runyon.

On December 27, 1971, the second annual winter concert was held in the Maysville High School Auditorium, featuring the Limestone Youth Orchestra, the Intermediate Orchestra, and the Beginning Strings, conducted by John K. Farris and me. On the program was a "Christmas Carol Medly" arranged by John K. Farris, played by the Beginning Strings; "Strings A-Struttin'," "Yultide Waltz," and "The Night Before Christmas," by Muller-Rusch, played by the Intermediate Orchestra; and "Sarabande and Allegro" by Corelli, "Concerto for Two Piccolos" by Vivaldi with Yvonne Rigdon and Ann Cooper as soloists, "A Christmas Fugue" arranged by Brown, "Prayer of St. Gregory" by Hovhaness, with Norman Yeager as trumpet soloist, "Latin Holiday" and "Yuletide Fantasy" by Muller, performed by the Limestone Youth Orchestra.

The string program was growing rapidly, in terms of interest by students, community awareness, and financial help. I was pleased to receive funds from the University of Kentucky to pay John K. Farris for his help with the program.

In March 1971, the Limestone Youth Orchestra was incorporated by the Kentucky Department of State as a non-stock organization. We were henceforth able to receive tax-free funds.

chapter twelve

String players from the orchestra accepted an invitation to perform at the North Central Regional Conference of the American String Teachers Association. The conference was held June 14-17, 1972, in Owensboro, Kentucky. The students attended the conference and played in a concert under the direction of Margery Aber from the University of Wisconsin. Miss Aber was an outstanding recognized authority on the Suzuki system of teaching music in America. The students participated in the Concert Orchestra conducted by Josef Klan. Several of our students were accepted, through auditions, for the Honors Orchestra, conducted by Harry Lantz, performing "Winter" from Vivaldi's "Four Seasons." It seemed unbelievable how far the string program had progressed in so short a time – students were playing this standard of the concert repertoire! We stayed in a dormitory at Brescia College and attended a reception given by the mayor of Owensboro where I was presented the key to the city.

In September 1972, the Limestone Youth Orchestra Board gave me a contract under which I would be paid $3,000 for the 1972-73 school year. I was to teach at least an hour five days a week before and after school at my discretion. The contract further stated that I would give necessary instruction to any and all persons who might so desire on behalf of the Limestone Youth Orchestra. I would in general serve

The LaMay String Quartet in a photo autographed for me: Ned, Bruce, Cathy and Rodney Farrar.

as a regular instructor, teacher, director of the orchestra's groups, and would aid the board of directors in the selection of scholarship benefits. I would provide and direct concerts as I deemed necessary.

I had long been interested in the Suzuki method of teaching violin by rote and had been privileged to hear Suzuki-trained 5-year-olds playing concertos in Atlanta. I had attended a workshop in Chicago in 1972 where Suzuki techniques were adapted for high school students. I had attended the Music Educators National Conference at the University of Tennessee, where Dr. William Starr and his Suzuki-trained children ages 5-12 gave a concert. They were just back from Venezuela, where critics had given them rave reviews. Margery Aber, renowned Suzuki specialist, had worked with my string students on Suzuki techniques in Owensboro, and I was hopeful that a Suzuki program could be started for pre-school children in Maysville. At our music camp in 1972 Kay Slone, head of the Suzuki Institute in Lexington, brought 12 of her students, three other teachers, and some of the parents, to demonstrate Suzuki methods for us. I continued my teaching with a modified form of Suzuki techniques, but insisted that the students read music from the beginning, rather than waiting for three years as the Suzuki school of teaching does.

The annual Christmas concert of the Limestone Youth Orchestra was held December 21, 1972, at the Maysville High School Auditorium and featured the Limestone Youth Orchestra, the Concert Orchestra, and the Limestone String Quartet. Members of the quartet were Karen Jones and C.J. Hunter, violins; Elizabeth Smart, viola; and Elaine Hansen, cello. The program included Purcell's "Minuet in G," McKay's Sinfonia No. 2, performed by the Concert Orchestra; Mozart's Fifth Quartet, K. 157, performed by the Limestone String Quartet; an Adagio and Allegro by Corelli, "Il Re Pastore" by Mozart, a Capriccio by Vivaldi, Berger's "Short Overture for Strings," Brown's "Christmas Fugue," and Muller's "Yuletide Festival," performed by the Limestone Youth Orchestra.

A concert climaxed the string camp of 1973 at the Mason County High School Band room. The camp was held at the home of Mr. and Mrs. Robert Browning and was co-sponsored by the orchestra board and the Kentucky Fine Arts Commission. Members of the LeMay

String Quartet of Lexington comprised the faculty. Members of the quartet were Bruce and Cathy Farrar, violins; Ned Farrar, viola; and Rodney Farrar, cello. The four also were members of the Lexington Philharmonic Orchestra.

Students attending camp were fortunate, indeed, to have such qualified instructors. There were daily private lessons for each student, group lessons, and a daily recital in the afternoon by the LeMay Quartet, both as a quartet, and as individual soloists.

Recreation included swimming, baseball and other outdoor activities. Swimming lessons were given to those who did not know how to swim prior to coming to camp. The swimming staff included Mrs. James Clarke, Mrs. William Chamness, Mrs. David Carpenter and Mrs. John Schmidt.

Ned Farrar was the guest conductor of the camp orchestra. Featured on the concluding concert were the members of the Suzuki class of beginners on violin taught by Cathy and Bruce Farrar, and the beginning viola class with Ned Farrar.

After the camp, I held string classes all summer beginning at 8 a.m. in the music room at Mason County.

In June 1973, four of our students attended the Institute for Strings and Chamber Music at the University of Kentucky. The institute, held June 11-29, offered classes in theory and humanities, private string lessons, performances with chamber groups, and work with the combined string orchestra. The four students who attended were Elaine Hansen, Sharon Thomas, C. J. Hunter, and Karen Jones. The director of the institute was Joseph Ceo. Karen Jones and Elizabeth Smart had attended the summer before.

Another marvelous experience for our students was the participation of C. J. Hunter, Karen Jones, Marla Wilson, and Elizabeth Smart in the Central Kentucky Youth Orchestra. This involved a great parental commitment for weekly Saturday rehearsals in Lexington, an hour away from Maysville.

On November 26, 1973, the Limestone Youth Orchestra presented a Baroque concert with Joseph Ceo as guest conductor, at the First Christian Church. Louise Mathews, newly-appointed string teacher in the Mason County Schools, Greg Collingsworth, and Wanda Majors, band director at Mason County High School, assisted with the program. The program featured Vivaldi's Concerto alla Rustica, Albioni's Sonata in C for Trumpet, Strings, and Continuo, Greg Collingsworth, soloist; Handel's Organ Concerto No. 4, James L. Clarke, soloist; Telemann's Concerto in G for Viola, Louise Mathews, soloist, and Suite in D Major for Trumpets, Oboes, Timpani, Strings and Continuo.

An experiment in teaching the Suzuki Method was started in the fall of 1974 at the Maysville Community College. John Semerin was the instructor of the class of children ages 3-5. A String Recital was held on March 18, 1974, with the older students, featuring works by by Bohm, Bach, Handel, Viotti, Telemann, Mozart, and Beutel.

In December 1976, I conducted the Limestone Youth Orchestra in a concert in the band room at Mason County. We played "God of Our Fathers" by Matesky, "Christmas Fugue" by Brown, "Holiday Tune" by Whitney, and "When Johnny Comes Marching Home" by Matesky. Members of the group included C. J. Hunter, concertmaster, Jeff Silvey, Mark Hook, Debbie Nichols, Priscilla Browning, and Sharon Thomas, first violins; Judy Robinson, principal, Cheryl Moss, Tawnya Crawford, Karen Silvey, second violins; Kelly Fritz, principal, John Zeigler, Chad Simms, violas; Joan Sapp, principal, Tami Crawford, Elain Hansen, Kevin Silvey, Karen Sapp, violoncellos; Todd Ritchie, Perry Moore, contrabass; Dana Poe, Kelly Allen, flutes; Renee Rigdon, oboe; Julia Moss, Jayne Johnson, clarinets; Cheryl Hodge, Lisa Muehlbauer, bassoon; Parker Grannis, Janet Lester, Leigh Moss, French horn; Tim Marinaro, Harold Hunt, Greg Taylor, trumpet; Dean Phelps, Steve Zweigart, trombone; Sherry Dearing, Kim Greene, saxophone; Danny Crawford, Clarkey Smith, tuba; Bino Manley, Myron Highfield, percussion; Lillina Crawford, librarian.

On December 12, 1976, I conducted the Chamber Orchestra in concert in the Mason County High School choral room. The program featured the Apollo Suite by Isaac, the Andante from Haydn's Surprise Symphony, Three German Dances by Haydn, Petit Tango by Kreichbaum, and "In Praise of Christmas" by Siennicki.

I was asked on several occasions to provide music at the Governor's Mansion in Frankfort, and I took a string ensemble that played several numbers as the guests were arriving. The occasion each time was the meeting held by the Preservation Committee in which awards were given for renovations of historical buildings in the state. We were stationed in an alcove between the twin staircases in the mansion. The visitors were always complimentary of the young musicians.

My method of recruitment for string players was very simple: whenever I found a student that watched me in chorus rehearsals with a steady gaze, I asked to see them after class. At this time I told the student that I wanted him to play the violin, viola, or cello. I told the student to ask their parents; if interested, I would furnish the instrument and provide the lessons. Two students stand out vividly who agreed to learn a stringed instrument: Elizabeth Smart and Sharon Thomas. I taught Elizabeth viola and promised her that if she would work hard, she would have a lot of fun and probably receive a college scholarship. As she learned to play the viola exceedingly well, she was a member of the Central Kentucky Youth Orchestra, a member of the Kentucky All-State Orchestra, a member of a string quartet that performed extensively, and received a scholarship to the College-Conservatory of Music, University of Cincinnati from which she graduated in 1977. (Little did I realize that she would become my daughter-in-law later!) Sharon Thomas became an excellent violinist and majored in strings at the University of Kentucky, taught in a string program in Danville, and headed a large string program at East Carolina University in North Carolina.

I am grateful for the training I received on the violin and I feel like the string program put all my violin training to good use. The Limestone Youth Orchestra brought much joy to many students and enriched their lives. Our little string program was also inspirational statewide. When we started the Limestone Youth Orchestra the only areas in Kentucky with similar programs were in large cities with universities: Lexington, Owensboro, Louisville. Now there are many more across the state, due perhaps in no small part to our efforts in Maysville.

Chapter 13:
The Limestone Chorale
"Play It Again"

Shortly after I resigned from the college, Marion Russell and Mary Milton Anderson, two of my most enthusiastic singers, came to me and urged me to start another chorus. They wanted to sing again! They insisted they would take care of all the details including recruitment of members and general management of the chorus. I agreed, appointed these two as choir managers, and the Limestone Chorale was born.

It is now more than 10 years old, and is a wonderful group of singers. Needless to say, the majority are former students of mine. The Chorale gives spring and holiday concerts each year; has sung with the Northern Kentucky Symphony Orchestra twice, has sung for each Rosemary Clooney Festival, and is the easiest group to teach I have ever had. We are supported financially by the Limestone Youth Orchestra Foundation, established in 1971. A dear friend interested in furthering the musical and fine arts opportunities for the community bequeathed more than $1 million to establish this non-stock organization. The generous gift provides funds to purchase music and to provide honorariums to out-of-town musicians who accompany the chorale in various concerts. No salaries are given to me, the conductor, or James L. Clarke, the accompanist; though substitutes for the two of us do receive remuneration for their services. The Foundation has established the Downing Academy for the Arts, where students may take private lessons in violin viola, cello, bass, piano, voice, organ, and classical guitar taught by professional musicians.

The Foundation also supports my newest musical endeavor, the Limestone Chamber Orchestra. This is a group of adults who "wanted to play again." I was urged for years to start an adult orchestra, and it came into being in 2002.

The Limestone Chorale's debut took place December 16, 1994, with a concert in the First Presbyterian Church. The Ledger-Independent devoted a full page with an article and color photographs of the new group:

chapter thirteen

Many new and familiar voices harmonize in Mason County's newest singing group, the Limestone Chorale

The choir has 40 members, including accompanist, James Clarke, who sings with the group on a cappella numbers. Director Coralie Runyon-Jones said she is excited by the overall quality of sound and the singers with whom she is working.

Newcomers include Bruce and Jean Hanna, Marvin Foltz, Mickey and Phil Wilson, and Shaun Reece. They are looking forward to the group's debut Friday, Dec. 16. "I'd like to sit and listen to the whole thing sometime," admitted Caroline Keller Reece. Caroline studied with Runyon-Jones at Mason County High School. "My dad had her here at Ripley High School, and my mom had her," she said, so her parents urged her to join the choir. "I was one of those lucky enough to be on the last European tour she did," Caroline said. When she came to her first Chorale rehearsal, a few of the songs were numbers she had performed before, "and it all came flooding back."

Music is more essential for Jean Hanna. The Hannas moved to Maysville this year when Bruce Hanna was appointed executive director of the Maysville Housing Authority. "I just can't imagine living without music," she said. "It's a big part of our lives. The other singers in the choir are a pleasure to sing with." Even though most are capable of being soloists, "they work real hard at blending and being a group."

"The amount and quality of musical talent in Maysville is just wonderful," Bruce Hanna said. He finds the rehearsals demanding. "The material is challenging. Coralie has a good sense of what's in the music. She's a superb conductor," he continued.

"I was in the very choir she took to Europe," said Mickey Wilson. She said the repertoire that appealed to the director had evolved over the years. Many of the other Chorale members had sung some of the music previously, so Mickey Wilson felt she had some catching up to do. She enjoys working in the ensemble, though. "Very close harmony is wonderful. I'm really enjoying being back in a group with such professionalism. I've always enjoyed Coralie's choice of music."

Runyon-Jones admits the program is heavily influenced by Anglican tradition, "because music is an important element in the church."

The first concert, "Sounds of Christmas," was sponsored by the Maysville-Mason County Arts Commission, and was as follows:

I:	Prelude: Variations on Christmas Carols	arr. Clarke
	James L. Clarke, organ	
	Heilig (double choir)	Mendelssohn
	In Dulci Jubilo	Old German Carol, arr. Pearsall
	O Clap Your Hands	Rutter
II:	Lord of the Dance	Shaker song, arr. Willocks
	Jesus Child	Rutter
	Blow, Blow, Thou Winter Wind	Rutter
	Shepherd's Pipe Carol	Rutter
	Stille Nacht	arr. Carter
	Birthday Carol	Willocks
III:	Gesu Bambino	Yon
	Michael Clarke, violin	
	A Lute Carol	Caldwell
	Ave Maria	Bach-Gounod
	Catherine Clarke, soprano	
IV:	A Boy Is Born	Britten
	A Maid Most Gentle	French Carol, arr. Carter
	In the Bleak Mid-Winter	Drake
	John Zeigler, tenor	
	Rocking	Czech Carol

chapter thirteen

    O Holy Night   arr. Rutter
    V: Joy to the World   arr. Kuykendald
    Scott Hanna and Cathie Curtis, trumpets; Brian Silvey,
    Charlie Ledford, trombone; Ben Faul, timpani

    Members of the chorus were: Sopranos: Leslie Ashby, Leslie Franklin, Paula Hendrickson, Jeanne Hanna, Bettsy Kalb, Evelyn McClanahan, Ann Scott Mason, Louanne Mattingly, Roseanne Palmer, Caroline Reece, Marion Russell, Marla Shadoan, Maggie Sledd, Genrose Turner, Mickey Wilson. Altos: Mary Anderson, Lennie Calland, Mary V. Clarke, Suellen Faris, Sheila Goldsmith, Suzan Haughaboo, Jewell Holland, Louise Moneyhan, Laura Rains, Bedouin Ullery, Betty Wood. Tenors: James L. Clarke, Kelly Clarke, Bill Courtney, Shaun Reece, Winn Turner, John Zeigler. Basses: Charles Clarke, Michael Clarke, Marvin Foltz, Bruce Hanna, Kent Kalb, Philip Wilson.

    The accompanist for the chorale is James L. Clarke, local attorney and an exceptional musician. Jim has been my accompanist for many years and is outstanding in every respect. He is a fine organist as well. He has a great talent for improvisation as well as for an accurate reading of the score. Two of his sons are attorneys, as well, and are excellent musicians, too. Both sing with the chorale and one is an excellent violinist with the chamber orchestra. Another son is a physician and was a charter member of the chorale and a daughter is a professional singer in New York City and often a soloist with the chorale. I really could not do without James L. Clarke, his sons Michael and Kelly, and his daughter Catherine.

    The year 1995 was very busy for the Limestone Chorale. Liz Magnes, jazz pianist, performed in the second half of the program. She is an international artist from Jerusalem and had been visiting her parents, Dr. and Mrs. Milton Rosenthal, in nearby Augusta. Liz had spent the last six months before her visit studying and performing in Paris, France. Playing jazz with percussion effects and Moroccan rhythms, she combined sounds with her hands and her fingers were everywhere on the piano.

    On June l, 1995, the Limestone Chorale held its spring concert at Trinity Methodist Church with James L. Clarke, organ, and piano, and with Bettsy Kalb, piano. The program follows:

Fantaisie in E Flat	Saint-Saens
James L. Clarke	
Quatre Motets sur des thèmes gregoriens	Duruflé
John Zeigler, Cantor	
Sicut cervus	Palestrina
Beati Quorum Via	Stanford
Carnaval, selections	Schumann
Bettsy Kalb, piano	
Four Robert Burns Ballads	Mulholland
Amazing Grace	Furnivall
Kelly Clarke, Tenor	
Down By the Riverside	Rutter
Let the People Praise Thee, O God	Mathias
Grieve Not the Holy Spirit of God	Noble
John Zeigler, tenor	
My Soul Doth Magnify the Lord	Rutter
I Was Glad When They Said Unto Me	Parry

The Limestone Chorale, 1994.

chapter thirteen

In October 1995, the chorale presented a concert at Philippus United Church of Christ, Cincinnati, Ohio, on its Fall Concert Series. The same choral selections were given as in the previous program. At the time, my son Randy was director of music and organist at Philippus.

The Christmas Concert was held on December 10, 1995, at the First Christian Church and was assisted by the Morehead University Faculty Quintet and the Morehead University Brass Choir, Jon Burgess, conductor. I conducted the program with James L. Clarke at the organ. The program featured "Three Christmas Carols," arranged by Harvey for brass quintet; "Missa Brevis" by Matthews; "Magnificat and Nunc Dimittis" by Sumsion; "Christmas Night," arranged by Rutter; "Sir Christmas" by Mathias; "In the Bleak Mid-Winter" by Darke; "Sans Days Carol" arranged by Rutter; "Lord of the Dance" arranged by Willocks; "Jesu, Joy of Man's Desiring" arranged by Willocks; a selection of carols in which the audience was invited to sing along; and "Arise, Your Light Has Come" by Danner.

By 1996 several new members joined the chorale: Kaye Browning, Cara Clarke, Charles Calvert, Sean Dennison, Basil Mattingly, C. J. Hunter, Phillip Manning, Andrew Wood, Marty Frankenhoff, John Denham, Lois Waldren, and Sheila Goldsmith.

For the 1996 spring concert I chose "100 Years of Broadway" by Mac Huff. and asked Dennison Keller to make this presentation special. Keller, a native of Ripley, is well known for his work with the Miss Ohio and Miss America Pageants. He also served as the talent coach and grooming advisor for Miss Ohio and two of those women became Miss America. He served as a judge of the 1992 Miss America Pageant in Atlantic City and has judged more than 300 pageants in 39 states. After my call to him to "fix the choir," he had two weeks to add choreography to make the show sparkle. It took a bit of urging, but the result was tremendous. The program was given at the Maysville Opera House and the orchestra was directed by Josh Dekaney, a senior music education student at the University of Kentucky and director of the Broadway All-Stars, an instrumental ensemble based in Lexington. He also was a member of the Lexington Philharmonic Orchestra.

Bettsy Kalb was at the piano, and I directed the orchestra and chorus. The house was packed and many were standing. The ovation was tremendous. Many people would not leave when the program was over – as if we would do it again if they stayed!

Martha Comer, the loyal and faithful reviewer of our concerts for the Ledger-Independent, reported that:

> "The Chorale's presentation was an evening to remember. When the best give their best, the result is one perfect evening of delight. That's how it was Friday night at the Opera Theater as Maysville's finest talent presented a concert of "100 Years of Broadway."
>
> There may have been one vacant seat in the house, but that was only because of latecomers who stood in the back.
>
> Not a moment lacked a graceful harmony as the Limestone Chorale sang classic favorites from "Give My Regards to Broadway" to a glorious finale "There's No Business Like Show Business,"
>
> Adding to the joy of the moments was the combo, "the Broadway All-Stars" with Bettsy Kalb at the piano.
>
> The seven-part program divided itself into selection such as "The Music of Tin Pan Alley," the great era of Rodgers and Hammerstein, and above all "The Golden Years." If you preferred "Hello, Dolly" to "Try to Remember," this may be what you remember most. Certainly the music from "Oklahoma" was star struck for the audience. And who could fail to mention "Seventy-six Trombones"?
>
> The music of Webber and Sondheim claimed its shining moment, after which the voices of the Limestone Chorale swung into contemporary Broadway.
>
> It was not a minute too long. Coralie Runyon Jones, concert master that she is, has an infallible touch for what is best, when to start, and when to say goodnight.
>
> Giving the evening the smoothness of good art was R. Dennison Keller, choreographer, and Josh Dekaney, of Houston, Texas, the orchestra's director."

On September 7, 1996, the Chorale performed with the Northern Kentucky Symphony in its presentation of "The War Between the States." The conductor of the Symphony, James R. Cassidy, had invited the chorus to participate in their Summer Park Series. He came to Maysville to work with the choir, and we rehearsed with the orchestra at NKU. The concert was repeated in Maysville on the lawn of the community college on September 9. It was a fine experience for my singers to have the opportunity to perform with a symphony orchestra, and we enjoyed it very much. This second presentation was sponsored by the Maysville-Mason County Arts Commission and was "Picnic with the Pops!"

In November 1996 one of my former students, Michael Bolden, and his wife Annie Cain Bolden, presented a recital in Fields Auditorium at the Maysville Community College. Michael was an outstanding student, and a member of the high school choir that went to England. He was only in the 8th grade, but I recognized the potential of his voice, and I wanted him to have that experience. Michael and Annie met when they were performers in the Stephen Foster Story in Bardstown, Kentucky. Michael was the choral teacher at Butler High School in Louisville, and Annie, a teacher of private voice lessons, and he were ministers of music in their church in Louisville. A highlight of their careers was a concert tour in Singapore. I was extremely proud of Michael and what he had done with his beautiful tenor voice. On the concert in Maysville, the chorale joined them in the Gounod "Sanctus."

On Sunday, December 15, 1996, the chorale presented a concert

The Limestone Chorale, 2005.

entitled "The Sounds of Christmas" at the First Christian Church. An instrumental ensemble provided accompaniment on several of the numbers, made possible by funds from the Gordon Lee and Elsie Downing Fund for the Arts. This source of financial support has made it possible for me to use professional musicians to enhance the choir's programs. The program featured "Hodie Christus Natus Est" by Sweelinck, "Justorum Animae" by Standord, "A Babe Is Born" by Mathias, "Christmas Day" by Holst, "For Us a Child Is Born," by Bach, "Lord of the Dance" arranged by Willocks, "There Is No Rose of Such Virtue" by Carocciolo, "Ave Maria" by Biebl; "The Christmas Song" arranged by Knight, and "O Holy Night" arranged by Rutter. The Chorale was accompanied by an instrumental ensemble of violins, violas, cello, flutes, oboes, clarinets, basson, and a French horn.

On May 23, 1997, the Limestone Chorale presented "A Night on Broadway" at the Opera Theater. The Jay Flippin Orchestra of Morehead provided the accompaniment, and Denny Keller was again the staging director. Three works were performed: Andrew Lloyd Webber's "Phantom of the Opera," arranged by Lojeski; Lucy Simon's "The Secret Garden," arranged by Lojeski; and "Classic Cole Porter," arranged by Mac Huff. New members joining the chorale were Naomi Curtis, Katie Davis, Tom Hamrick, Mary Manning, and George Moore.

The Christmas concert featured father and daughter, as Catherine, "Cacey" Clarke joined the chorale as soprano soloist on December 22, 1997, at Trinity Methodist Church. Her father, James L. Clarke, opened the concert with Saint-Saens's "Prelude and Fugue in E Flat." We presented "Te Deum" by Haydn; "Come, Thy Holy Paraclete" by Hurd; "Ave Maria" by Biebl; "My Soul Doth Magnify the Lord" by Rutter; "Jesus, Jesus, Rest Your Head," "What Songs Were Sung," "The Carol of the Birds," and "I Wonder As I Wander" by Niles; "O Holy Night" by Adam; "The Many Moods of Christmas" by Shaw and Bennett, and "Sleigh Ride" by Anderson. The audience was invited to a reception after the concert by Mr. and Mrs. Phil Wilson at their home, Buffalo Trace, on Hillcrest.

On Sunday, March 22, 1998, the chorale presented the Requiem by John Rutter at the First Presbyterian Church. Soloists were Leslie Franklin and Naomi Curtis. An instrumental ensemble accompanied it, composed of Randolph Runyon, flute; Ben McKlveen, oboe; Suanne Blair, cello; Jane Zopff, harp; Frank Oddis, tympani; Suzanne Haughaboo, bells; Bettsy Kalb, organ.

The Christmas concert on Sunday, December 20, 1998, featured an instrumental ensemble and violin soloist, with James L. Clarke at the organ. The program included "Hail Gladdening Light" by Wood; "Te Deum" by Rutter; "O Nata Lux" by Lauridsen; "The Lord Is Shepherd" by Rutter, "Lord of the Dance" by Willcocks; "Carols of Christmas" by Mulholland; "Sonata in A" by Handel, with Leo Blair, violin; "Christmas Day" by Holst; "Candelight Carol" by Rutter; and "O Holy Night" by Adam, arranged by Rutter.

The spring concert on May 21, 1999, was presented at the Opera Theater. Suzan Haughaboo was the accompanist. The program: "Sing Praises" by Pfautsch; "The Sprig of Thyme" and "Birthday Madrigals" by Rutter; "Old Time Religion" by Hogan, "Wake Me Up, Lord" by Brown; "Ain't Got Time to Die" by Johnson; and "When Peace like a River" arranged by Groetenhuis. New members joining the the chorale were Eric Jackson, Jenny Jenkins, and David Sugarbaker.

The Christmas concert of 1999 was held in the beautiful sanctuary of St. Patrick Church on December 19 at 5 p.m. James L. Clarke was the accompanist and guest organist was Zach Ullery (son of my longtime student Bedouin) who opened the concert with Bach's "Prelude and Fugue in G Major." The chorale then formed into a double choir for "Buccinate in Neomenia Tuba" by Croce. This was followed by the Puccini "Gloria" with John Zeigler as tenor soloist. The rest of the program included "In the Bleak Mid-Winter" by Darke; "I Wonder As I Wander" arranged by Rutter; "Go, Tell It on the Mountain" arranged by Jennings; and "The Many Moods of Christmas" by Shaw and Bennett. Megan Zeigler and Bobby Boone were new members of the chorale.

A Lenten concert was presented at St. Patrick Church, and I asked John Zeigler, my colleague and former student, to share in conducting duties. I also asked my student Robert Boone to train the choir for a number and to conduct it. John Zeigler, a member of the chorale and a well-known tenor soloist, began his musical training at the age of 10 as a member of the Cincinnati Boy Choir. After returning to Maysville, he was my student at Mason County where I taught him voice as well as composition. He excelled in both areas and attended Morehead State University. He was a student of James Ross Beane and performed with the Lexington Singers and the Louisville Bach Society. As a conductor, John has held several positions in Maysville, including at the First Christian Church, First Baptist Church, and Central United Methodist Church. He was the director of the combined church choirs at the first Cameron Mills Praise Service. He became a valued member of the Maysville Players, appearing in "The Music Man" and Sondheim's "Into the Woods." He was also featured in the Maysville Community College's production of "Godspell." He is a valued employee of Emerson Electric, and conducts a private studio, teaching voice, piano, and composition. His wife, Barbara, teaches choral music in the Mason County Schools and also teaches private lessons in piano.

Bettsy Hensley Kalb, another one of my very excellent piano students, served as the accompanist for the concert.

The program was as follows:

Ubi Caritas	Duruflé
Marty Frankenhoff, cantor	
Tenebrae factae sunt	Haydn
conducted by Robert Boone	
Grieve Not the Holy Spirit of God	Noble
John Zeigler, tenor	
Requiem	Fauré

Kent Kalb, baritone; Megan Zeigler and Sung-Young Lee, sopranos; Kelly Clarke, baritone, John Zeigler, Conductor
A new member of the choir was Holly McElfresh.

In 1995 the first annual Rosemary Clooney Festival was held, with proceeds to benefit the restoration of the Russell Theater in downtown Maysville. Various organizations were asked to perform on September 25 for an all-day celebration of one of Maysville's most famous citizens. The day's activities were climaxed by a dinner served at beautifully appointed round tables set up in the middle of the street. A large bandstand was erected on Market and Third Streets where Rosemary and her orchestra performed. The Limestone Chorale appeared twice on the program; the first at 2 p.m. in the lobby of the French Quarter Hotel and the second at 9:15 p.m. in front of the Russell Theater. It was on this spot that my Civic Chorus performed for the world premiere of Rosemary's movie, "The Stars Are Singing" more than 50 years earlier.

For the second year's festival, the chorale was invited to give a concert in the Opera Theater, and we have done so each year since. In 2004 the theater was undergoing renovation, and the concert was held outside in an area designated as Picnic in the Parking Lot. Each concert in the theater has drawn overflowing crowds. The most memorable audience was the one from the excursion paddlewheel boat that delayed leaving Maysville until the concert in the Opera Theater was over! Even the second balcony, dusty as it was, was filled!

For the second concert I asked Cacey Clarke to be the producer of the show, and she had some great ideas for making it a hit. We repeated portions of "100 Years of Broadway" with other popular selections. James Clarke was the marvelous accompanist on a Yahama electric piano that had been purchased the previous year. Soloists were Patty Graves, Mary Anderson, Laura Rains, Michael Clarke, Kaye Browning, Marion Russell, Charles Calvert, Roseanne Palmer, Cacey Clarke, Kelly Clarke, Holly Kimball, Genrose Turner, John Zeigler, Bedouin Ullery, Louanne Mattingly, Megan Zeigler, Leslie Franklin, and Mickey Wilson.

In 2001 I made a rapid change in the program for the Clooney Festival: September 11 had just occurred, and it did not seem appropriate to do the program as planned. I had arranged for Chuck Gillespie, baritone, from Columbus, Ohio, to be a guest on the program. I immediately called him and together we planned a program that would be "A Tribute to America." Chuck, a TV personality in weather forecasting, has a beautiful voice and performs in Columbus in countless musicals, shows and church affairs. He is also a native of Maysville and the son of my bridge-playing friend, Margaret Ann Gillespie. The program turned out to be fitting and appropriate. James Clarke, Kristen Carlson, and Linda Ford provided the accompaniments. Soloists in addition to Chuck were Kelly Clarke and Patti Graves. New members of the chorale for this program were Mary Jo Baker, Gisela Carlson, Karen Cox, Patty DeVaughan, Ben Jones, Brian King, Sean McErlane, Mike Meyer, Moira O'Neil, and Chris Waits.

In 2002 the program given for the festival was one of nostalgia and sadness. Rosemary Clooney, who loved her hometown, Maysville, and always promoted it in many ways, had performed at each of the festivals named for her, had died. The chorale performed "A Tribute to Rosemary." One of the highlights were the songs that Rosemary had made famous, sung by Chuck Gillespie. He had thrilled the overflow audience the previous year, and we were pleased to invite him back for this concert. Catherine Clarke was another featured guest soloist, and she sang a medley of Gershwin songs. The Gershwins were neighbors of Rosemary in Hollywood. Another close friend of "our girl singer" was Bob Hope. Our choir managers, Marion Russell and Mary Anderson, had set new words to the famous star's theme song: "Thanks for the Memory." The chorale's presentation of it brought tears to the eyes of the Clooney family, seated in the front row of the Opera Theater. James Clarke was the accompanist for the choir and Susan Cairns of Columbus accompanied Chuck in his selections. The chorale opened the program with "How Can I Keep From Singing" and closed with "Every Time We Say Goodbye." New singers joining us were Keith Boyd, Cathy Insko, Leigh Rains, and Saundra Stevens.

For the 2003 festival, the chorale repeated its old standby, "100 Years of Broadway" at the Opera Theater on September 20. New members joining were Toni McHugh and Richard Zeigler.

The 2004 observance was held in the parking lot adjacent to the theater. James Clarke entertained the large crowd with his piano selections and George Brown of West Union, Ohio, provided additional accompaniment on guitar and bass for the chorale. We sang "Down by the Riverside" arranged by Rutter; "Take My Hand, Precious Lord" arrnged by Lojeski; "Order My Steps" by Schrader"; "Old Time Religion" by Hogan; "Praise His Holy Name" by Hampton; "Thanks for the Memory" arranged by Emerson; and a Rodgers and Hammerstein medley. New members of the chorale were Carolyn Least, Tonya Castle, Tami Conrad, Krissie Clarke, Tim Waits, Randall Dennison, Craig Weber, and Andrew Young.

John Zeigler conducted the Christmas concert on Sunday, December 17, 2000, in St. Patrick's Church: "O Magnam Mysterium" by Herman; "Ave Maria" by Busto; "Missa Brevis" by Leavitt; and "The

Many Moods of Christmas" by Shaw-Bennett.

I conducted the spring concert on Sunday, April 22, 2001, at the First Presbyterian Church. After an organ prelude played by my son, Randolph Runyon, the Limestone Brass played a group of selections. Included were "Creation Fanfare" by Edwards and "Guide Me, O Thou Great Jehovah" by Hughes, arr. by Montgomery. The chorale then presented "The Creation" by Haydn. Soloists were Paula Walton, John Zeigler, and Bruce Hanna. Accompanists were Amber Lee Abel and Kristen Carlson, advanced piano students of mine.

I directed the Christmas concert of 2001 at St Patrick's Church with James Clarke at the organ and piano and with James Culp, classical guitarist. The program featured carols from around the world. Catherine Clarke sang "Gesu Bambino" by Yon, "I Wonder As I Wander" by Niles, and "Ave Maria" by Bach-Gounod.

James Clarke presented a medley of Christmas carols and this was followed by the chorale singing "O Come, O Come, Emmanuel," "Angels We Have Heard on High," "Away in a Manger," "Ding Dong, Merrily on High," "The Angel's Carol" by Rutter, "The Friendly Beasts, "A la Nanita Nana," "This Christmastide' by Fraser, "Go Where I Send Thee" arranged by Hogan with Kelly Clarke as baritone soloist, and "The Many Moods of Christmas" by Shaw-Bennett.

The Limestone Chamber Orchestra joined with the chorale on the Christmas concert held December 22, 2002, at the First Christian Church. The orchestra, a group of adults, had played together for a few months, and joined the Bell Choir in an arrangement of "Good Christian Men, Rejoice." John Zeigler had arranged the number as well as the carols that were performed with the choir, congregation and orchestra. The Benjamin Britten "Ceremony of Carols" was performed by the chorale with Megan Zeigler as soloist. After the carols, the chorale concluded the concert with "What Sweeter Music" by Rutter and two numbers with orchestral accompaniment: "Candlelight Carol" and "O Holy Night," arranged by John Rutter. Leslie Fox was the soprano soloist in the last number.

Two new members joined the chorale for this concert: Rumulo Connsumo and Barbara Winborn. Dr. Comsumo, a native of the Philippines, was a teacher of mathematics in St. Patrick School, and

Mrs. Winborn was the wife of the rector of the Church of the Nativity. The members of the Chamber Orchestra were Cathy Insko, Yuting Hsaio, Keith Boyd, Saundra Stevens, violins; Steve Moss, Marla Brock, John Zeigler, violas; Mary Dawn Fulton, cello. The members of the Bell Choir were Greg Brock, Marla Brock, Sue Ellen Grannis, Pat Graves, and Jackie Hall

On Palm Sunday, April 13, 2003, the Limestone Chambers Orchestra and the Limestone Chamber Singers presented an outstanding concert at the First Presbyterian Church. The orchestra played the Overture to Don Giovanni by Mozart; Arioso by Bach; Concerto in G by Huber (Cathy Insko, soloist); Suite by Leclair; Sonata in F: Allegro by Beethoven (Yuting Hsiao, soloist); Divertimento no. 2 in D Major: Allegro by Mozart. The Chamber Singers presented Schubert's Mass in G by Schubert with soloists Leslie Fox, soprano; Cathy Insko, soprano; Marty Wallingford, tenor, John Zeigler, tenor, and David Sugarbaker, bass.

Cathy Insko is the concertmistress of the orchestra and is an excellent violinist. She was my pupil in middle school and high school. She is very talented and plays and sings with a band. Her band recently gave a benefit concert for a desperately ill child and raised $11,000 in one night's performance. Yuting Hsaio is a superb violinist and a graduate of Taiwan University. She lives in Maysville and is associated with the China Garden Restaurant.

On June 29, 2003, the chorale presented Fauré's Requiem at the First Presbyterian Church. Larry Keenan, professor of organ at Morehead State University, presented a program on the newly installed organ and served as the accompanist for the Requiem. Soloists were Megan Zeigler, soprano and Noel Weaver, baritone. Megan, daughter of John Zeigler, has a beautiful soprano voice and is majoring in music at Kentucky Wesleyan College in Owensboro. Noel Weaver is director of choral activities at Ballard High School in Louisville. His choirs have performed throughout the United States and abroad. He is married to the former Melissa Turner, one of my most outstanding vocal students. Their son, Aaron, an outstanding cellist at the University of Kentucky, frequently plays with the Limestone Chamber Orchestra.

The chorale and chamber orchestra presented a Christmas

concert, "The Joys of Christmas," on Sunday, December 14, 2003, at the First Presbyterian Church. James L. Clarke accompanied the chorale and played magnificent arrangements on the new organ at the church. The Chamber Orchestra played "Jesu, Joy of Man's Desiring" by Bach; "Lo, How a Rose E'er Blooming" arranged by Goldsmith; and Pachelbel's Canon. The chorale sang "A Babe Is Born" by Mathias, "Ave Maria" by Busto, "The Lord of the Dance" arranged by Willocks, "This Christmastide" by Fraser, "Christmas Lullabye" and "Angel's Carol" by Rutter, "Go, Tell It on the Mountain" arranged by Jennings, and "We Wish You a Merry Christmas" arranged by Warpell. New members of the chorale were Tonya Castle and Patrick Estill. Joining the orchestra were Tara Hester, Jennifer Stanfield and Aaron Weaver.

The spring concert was held on May 22, 2004 at the Presbyterian Church and featured a family twosome: Zachary Ullery, organ, and his mother, Bedouin Ullery, who accompanied the chorale at the piano. Zach is an outstanding graduate of the University of Kentucky School of Music with a degree in organ, voice, and music education. He is the director of choral activities at Clark County High School in Winchester, Kentucky, and the assistant organist at the Church of the Good Shepherd in Lexington. The chorale sang "How Can I Keep from Singing," "Grace" by Hayes, "Praise His Holy Name" by Hogan, "All My Trials" by Luboff, and "Order My Steps" by Burleigh. The Erin Ways, an instrumental group specializing in Celtic music from Cincinnati, performed three numbers, and provided the accompaniment for the "Missa Criolla" by Ramirez, Marty Frankenhoff, tenor. Colin Faris joined the chorale as a new member.

A Christmas concert was held Dec. 12, 2004, at the First Presbyterian Church to an overflow crowd. Featured on the concert was Catherine Clarke. Choral selections included Rachmaninoff's "Ave Maria," Clarence Dickinson's 'The Shepherds' Story," Vivaldi's Gloria, and Holst's "Christmas Day."

The Limestone Chorale has now been performing for 10 years and continues to be the finest choral organization I have had the joy of conducting. Its members are dedicated, loyal, and exceedingly good musicians. I think back over 64 years of desiring perfection in my endeavors in music, and this singing group represents the culmination of that desire.

The Limestone Chamber Orchestra, now two years old, is a small group of string players who yearned to "play again." Some were members of the Limestone Youth Orchestra of the 1970s. New members include George Brown, from West Union, Ohio; and Saundra Stevens, also from West Union. Another fine addition is Tyler Mains, a ninth-grade student at the Mason County High School and a student in violin at the Downing Academy of Music. He was in the Cadet Orchestra at Maple Mount that I conducted, and I knew that he would excel. His eagerness and enthusiasm for music were well evident. Another newcomer to the group is a high school student violinist, Amy Holbrook, from Seaman, Ohio.

I am still teaching many of the same students, their children, and even their grandchildren. My chorale, orchestra and private students give me great joy, and cause me to still dream dreams of high goals in perfecting the music we have inherited from the masters of the past and present.

Chapter 14:
St. Michael's and St. Patrick's
"Recapitulation: Students and Children of Students"

I agreed to teach music at St. Michael's Parochial School in the fall of 1997. It was a part-time position – mornings only – and I had a marvelous time doing it. I had taught the 7th and 8th grade music there in the '50s when I taught in the Ripley schools. I had fond memories of the nuns who taught there, and I was warmly received by the principal, Sister Rosemary Winklejohannus, as well as Father Feldhaus. Sister Rosemary was highly educated – she had studied in Germany – and had high standards for her students. She arranged a suitable and pleasant music nook in the cafeteria where the children in kindergarten through the 6th grade came for their music sessions. I taught them sight singing using the Kodaly system. It was successful, and I was pleased. I also taught the recorder in the upper grades the second year that I was there. We played Christmas carols in harmony and performed in the lobbies of the two banks in town on one occasion. We also performed in a lovely church built by German immigrants who had settled in that area many years before.

I taught the children the operetta, "Over the Rainbow" and we performed it in the parish church. The play was successful and a large audience attended.

After the second year I had agreed to teach at St. Patrick School in Maysville, and both jobs were a bit much. I enjoyed thoroughly my two years at St. Michael's, but now turned my attention to developing a strong music program in the Catholic schools of Maysville.

Scott Poe, one of my singers in the choirs over the years, called me in the summer of 1998 and said he wanted me to meet the new principal of St. Patrick School. At the appointed time I did meet Jay Jacobs, and his secretary, Helen Powers. I was impressed with Mr. Jacobs and was convinced that I should take on another part-time teaching position. As the years have unfolded, Jay and Helen and her husband, John, have become close friends. The years I taught at St. Pat have been exceedingly happy years for me.

Only five students had enrolled in chorus, and we met in the basement, under the altar of St. Patrick's Church. Only five, but how outstanding they were: Allison Poe, Michael Waits, Eli Thomas, Annie Gay Van Meter, and Amy Gill. After a day or two, I insisted on more students and more students came. I got them from study halls, before school at 7 a.m., at noon, and any other time I could. Mr. Jacobs was tremendously cooperative, and we found ways of enlarging the choir.

I took 22 students to the choral clinic at Morehead University, and three of them won the solo competition to perform on the closing night's concert: Michael Waits, Eli Thomas, and Allison Poe

I worked with the 7th and 8th grades and by Christmastime, we had a concert ready with three choruses: the 53-voice 7th and 8th grade choir, the 25-voice St. Patrick Chorale, and the 61-voice high school choir. The concert took place in the St. Patrick Church on December 17, 1998, with James L. Clarke and Amber Lee Abel, a 7th grade student and piano pupil of mine, as accompanists. The program featured, "Come, Let Us Sing" by Lindth, "Lullabye of the Dove" by Besig, "To the Glory of Our King" by Leaf, "Te Deum" by Haydn, "Now God Be Praised" by Vulpius, "Christmas Lullaby" by Rutter, "Ding, Dong, Merrily on High" by Near, "Let the Praise Go 'Round" by Boyce, and "O Holy Night" by Adam.

In the spring the choirs gave an exciting concert entitled "On With the Show!" Mark Thomas, former director of the Children's Theater in Lexington, and the father of Eli, was the producer of the show and brought out the very best in lighting and staging. Dinner was served and the program followed. There was a sold-out audience, and it was a lot of fun and a great success. James L. Clarke and Amber Lee Abel were the accompanists again. Entertainment during the dinner hour was presented by Bedouin Ullery, James L. Clarke, and Bettsy Kalb. The 7th and 8th grade choir sang "America, of Thee I Sing" by Donnelly and Strid and "Chariot's Comin'" by Busig and Price. The St. Patrick Choir sang selections from "The Phantom of the Opera" by Webber-Lojeski and "A Century of Song" by Irving Berlin. The St. Patrick Singers sang "Ain't-a That Good News" by Dawson, "Wake Me Up, Lord" by Brown, "Plenty Good Room / Sit Down, Servant" by DeCormier, "A City Called Heaven" by Poelinitz, and "Down by the

Riverside" by Rutter

The concert was held in the school gymnasium, which had been transformed into a concert hall by the committee in charge of the concert. Four hundred people attended this benefit concert and nearly $5,000 was raised for the school's tuition assistance program. An anonymous item in the Comment Line of the Ledger-Independent was very complimentary on the evening's program: "My, oh my, what a delightful time we had at the St. Patrick gymnasium on Thursday evening. The food, the decorations, the hard work of the adults responsible for this wonderful program, the conductor, the producer, the accompanist, and most especially, the music of the students, made for a truly wonderful evening."

I resigned from St. Patrick School in 1999 because I was discouraged about the low enrollment. In order to have a good choir, I had to teach some at 7 a.m., some at noon, and some after school. I had only had five enrolled in the beginning though I did have a fairly large group at the end of the year for our concert. I enjoyed teaching there, loved the teachers and administration, but had my hands full outside of school: I was teaching private lessons in voice, violin, and piano at home four days a week. I was also driving to Morehead every other Tuesday to take violin lessons from Leo Blair because I wanted to keep in shape on the violin, my first love.

After my resignation, one of my former students, Paula Henderson Walton, took the position. She had just graduated from Eastern Kentucky University with a degree in music. She was succeeded by Tom Hamrich, who had just retired from a very successful teaching career in the Manchester, Ohio, high school.

After a period of time though and much persuading on the part of the Principal Jacobs, I agreed to go back to St. Patrick. As a means of inducement he arranged that I would have every student in the high school in chorus! I thought this was an opportunity too grand to pass up. Imagine, every student in the high school! That would take care of recruitment! Some of the students did not want to be told they had to take music, but at the time I thought I could easily win them over. It was quite a task to teach every student in the high school: sharing the music was a problem; having the chairs set up for the rehearsal;

keeping all of them interested. Three teachers were assigned to each rehearsal, and they endeavored to help with discipline and made out the grades accordingly. All I had to do was teach. We succeeded in having a wonderful concert at Christmas and in the spring. We had to use seven risers, and several students had to stand on the floor. I even brought in the 7th and 8th graders to join the large chorus for the final number, Rutter's "The Lord Bless You and Keep You." I took several students to the choral clinic at Morehead State University, but had the misfortune to fall and break my right leg! It was not a bad break, but enough to keep me away from teaching for a short while.

As I was filing music, arranging chairs, and getting ready for the all-high school chorus, Mr. Jacobs came to the room to tell me that the World Trade Center had been attacked by planes and the nation was steeped in sorrow and fear. It was Sept. 11, 2001. All classes were suspended, and the students and teachers watched the televised news of the unfolding events. On Friday, September 14, a call came to the school to see if I could provide a chorus to sing on the courthouse lawn at a prayer service. I immediately called in the 7th and 8th grade students and taught them "God Bless America." Linda Ford, the elementary vocal and high school band instructor, accompanied them on a portable keyboard. In just a short while we walked to the site where many people had gathered for the prayers offered for the ones who were in the path of danger and for the safety of America. After the chorus sang the first verse of the well-known song, I asked the audience to join in. There were choked voices and sobs heard as the people joined in the singing of this patriotic number. I was very proud of my choristers. In their navy and plaid uniforms, their white shirts, the young people conducted themselves in a solemn and beautiful manner.

On December 13, 2001, the bands and choruses of St. Patrick presented "The Sounds of Christmas" in the newly renovated school gymnasium. Since I had taught there in 1998-1999, the school had undergone a major building program. There was a new high school building with a large choral and band room on the third floor and an elevator installed! It was quite a change from the choral room I had had under the church! The gymnasium made a wonderful concert hall after Ann Waits, with her marvelous decorating ability, had finished with it.

The Limestone Youth Orchestra Foundation had been generous to my requests for help with the music program, and we had a Yamaha electric piano, and those seven sets of risers. Kristen Carlson and Amber Lee Abel were the accompanists for the choral part of the program and John McHugh, a high school student, assisted on the guitar. The St. Patrick Mixed Chorus sang "Now God Be Praised" by Vulpius, "Precious Lord, Take My Hand" arranged by Lojeski, and "O Holy Night" by Adam. The St. Patrick Chorale presented Bach's cantata "For Us a Child Is Born." The Middle School Choir sang "Come, Let Us Sing" by Lindlh, "Panis Angelicus" by Franck, "Lullabye of the Dove" by Besig, "Inscription of Hope" by Stroope, "Ding, Dong, Merrily on High" by Near, "'Twas the Night Before Christmas" by Simeone, "Toumba ta Toumba," "O Come, All Ye Faithful," "Joy to the World," and "Silent Night."

It is obvious from the program that the Middle School Choir was a remarkable group. I do not believe I have ever had the privilege of teaching such outstanding 7th and 8th graders. It seemed they could learn anything I placed before them.

I was fortunate to have an assistant, Mickey Wilson, one of my former high school and college students. Mickey walked into the classroom one day, and said she would like to help me! She said she would file the music, arrange the chairs, etc. Before long, I had her conducting some of the numbers, and she had a good time working with me and the students.

Every student from grades 7-12 was in the choruses. I really believe that is how music should be taught in the schools.

The new owner of the Ford Motor Company in Maysville, a Mr. Nourse, asked me if I could provide a chorus to sing for a party he was giving for his employees. I chose the Middle School Choir for this occasion. It was held at the French Quarter Hotel. Just before Santa Claus entered, they sang "The Night Before Christmas." The party was held after school had been dismissed for the holidays, and I was proud that my students gave of their time for this occasion. Mr. Nourse gave a check for $200 for the music program. Mickey helped me and conducted the group in one of their numbers. Mr. Jacobs brought the newly purchased keyboard and its very heavy speaker.

The Middle School Choir also gave a mini-concert for the passengers on the Mississippi Queen, a stern-wheeler passenger boat that docked frequently at Maysville. The 400 passengers who hailed from California, New York and many other places were returning to the boat after having toured the town and Old Washington. We took a keyboard down to the riverside. Mickey directed the group; I played the accompaniment, and the passengers formed a receptive crowd on the bank as the children sang. I taught them "Down the O-hi-o," "My Old Kentucky Home," and several patriotic songs for the occasion.

A meaningful event occurred in February of 2002, when the Middle School Choir had an all-day clinic culminating in a concert in St. Patrick's Church. Julie Ann White was the choral clinician for the event. Julie was a dear friend of mine and a member of the faculty of the Maple Mount Music Camp where I had taught for a number of years. Julie was nationally known for her exceptional work with young

The kids singing "down by the riverside."

singers and her group had recently performed in New York's Carnegie Hall. The next year her group performed in the Pacific Rim Festival in Hawaii. Her husband, James Douglas White, a concert violinist and director of the Maple Mount Camp, performed as well. The program featured "Sing and Be Joyful" by Wilson, "Panis Angelicus" by Franck, "Gloria Tibi" from Leonard Bernstein's Mass, "Inscription of Hope" by Stroope, "Be Thou My Vision arranged by Shaw, "Gonna Rise Up Singin" and "Soon I Will Be Done" arranged by Emerson, "Can I Ride?" arranged by Shaw and Moore, and "Rhythm of Life" by Coleman.

On May 8, 2002, Linda Kern-Ford, the instrumental instructor at St. Pat, and I joined forces in a concert. After the elementary and high school bands performed, the Middle School Choir presented several numbers from the choral clinic held in February. I added a new group, the Girls' Chorus. In addition to some of the selections listed above from the clinic, the Girls' Chorus performed "For the Beauty of the Earth" by Rutter and "The Water Is Wide" arranged by Zanielli, the High School Chorus performed selections from "Godspell" arranged by Leyden, and all the choruses combined to sing "The Lord Bless You and Keep You" by Rutter.

In the fall of 2002 students could elect chorus instead of being required to take it. I still had a good number in the choir, though more manageable in terms of copies of music needed. The joint Christmas concert was held with the band and choruses. The Middle School Chorus was quite good again, and the High School Chorus was much easier to teach. I felt that all students were enjoying being in the choir. Mr. Jacobs asked me if I would teach art appreciation along with the choral work. I enjoyed this and worked hard to teach my students about the world's great artists and their painting. In the spring we took the entire high school to the Cincinnati Symphony Orchestra for a Friday morning concert, then lunch and a tour at the Cincinnati Art Museum.

In the choral portion of the Christmas concert the Middle School Choir sang "Sing for Joy" by Handel, "Adoramus Te" by Crocker, "Carol of the Bells" arranged by Liebergen, "Panis Angelicus" by Franck, and "Let the Praise Go 'Round" by Boyce; the High School Chorus sang "The Angel Carol" by Rutter, and the combined choruses sang "Carols of Christmas" by Mulholland.

On February 21, 2003, we had a second choral clinic, again with Julie Ann White as clinician. It was another wonderful event, and the students gave a beautiful program in the church. The "Panis Angelicus" had become such a favorite by students and teachers alike that we included it every chance we could. The program was given at 5 p.m., with Amber Lee Abel as the accompanist. We sang "Kyrie" by Dwyer/Ellis, "Panis Angelicus" by Franck, "Watters Ripple and Flow" arranged by Boshkoff, "Haida" arranged by McRae, "One Light" by Marcus/Schram, "Shine on Me," "Sing Hallelu, and "Lay Your Healing Hands on Me" arranged by Dillworth, "The Merry Heart of Stephen Foster" arranged by Kirk, and "My Old Kentucky Home" by Foster.

At the spring concert the Middle School Choir opened the choral part of the concert with "Kyrie" by Dwyer, "They Shall Soar like Eagles" by Manza, "Shine on Me" by Dilworth, "Waters Ripple and Flow" arranged by Boskhoff, "Ave Maria" by Schubert, and "Lay Your Healing Hands on Me" by Dilworth. The Girls' Chorus then sang "The Ash Grove" arranged by Dwyer. The High School Choir sang "Let the Praise Go 'Round" arranged by Hopson, "Ain't-a That Good News" and "God's Gonna Set the World on Fire" arranged by Hogan, and "When the Trumpet Sounds" by Thomas." Then the combined choirs sand "The Lord Bless You and Keep You" by Rutter.

On the winter concert of December 4, 2003, I used three of our outstanding pianists to accompany the choirs or perform solos. Tim Waits, an outstanding pianist and a ninth grade student, played the Allegro from Mozart's Sonata in C Major to open the choral part of the joint concert with the bands. The Middle School Choir presented "Alleluia" by Bach, "Carol of the Bells" by Leontovich, and "Sing and Be Joyful" by Wilson. The High School Choir sang "Gloria in Excelsis" by Vivaldi, "Nativity Carol' by Rutter, "Ev'ry Time I Feel the Spirit" arranged by Hogan, and "Take My Hand, Precious Lord" arranged by Lojeski. The combined choirs sang "O Holy Night" by Adam. Other student accompanists were Kathryn Ford and Amber Lee Abel.

In the spring of 2004, I was asked if I would do another gala like the one I did my first year at St. Pat. I agreed, and the event was tremendous. Before the program everyone gathered in the school cafeteria, where there were beautifully appointed tables of hors d'oeuvres, desserts, and a coffee bar. Background music provided by Carolyn Morris, Courtney Prichard, Beth Nolder, Kelsey Clarke, Kathryn Ford, and Sarah Watson, added to the festive atmosphere.

The music began at 7:30 p.m. Mr. Jacobs had built portable stages behind the risers and at the foot of the stage. Individual acts were presented in several locations and gave an exciting change from the usual programming. The Middle School Choir, which now included the 6th grade, opened the program with "Sing and Dance, Children of God" by Bedford. This was followed by "One Light" by Marcus and Schram. Adrianne Dodson sang "Tomorrow" by Strouse. The choir concluded its set with "In That Great Gettin' Up Morning" by Ellers. Carolyn Morris, a 7th grader, and Courtney Prichard, an 8th grader, were the accompanist for this part of the program.

After several numbers by the band students, Tim Waits played "Tarantella" by Pieczonka and Wade Hook performed the Bach "Toccata in D Minor." Tim is an exceptionally fine pianist. He studies at the Downing Academy of Music. Wade is the organist and choir director for his church. The rest of the program included "Order My Steps" by Buleigh, arranged by Schrader; "You'll Never Walk Alone" by Rodgers; "Take My Hand, Precious Lord," arranged by Lojenski; "I Wanna Be Ready," arranged by Powell, "God's Gonna Set This World on Fire," arranged by Hogan, and selections from "The Phantom of the Opera" by Webber-Lojeski.

Singing on the courthouse lawn.

I had been so fortunate to have Amber Lee Abel as my accompanist. She started taking piano from me when she was four years old. I knew that she would become an excellent pianist, and when she had studied for several years I urged her parents and grandparents to send her to study with a master teacher. She did so at Northern Kentucky University. In previous years I had had Kristen Carlson as my accompanist at St. Patrick School. She had also studied with me since she was in elementary school. She is an unbelievably gifted pianist and at this time she was studying at the University of Kentucky on scholarship.

The emcee for the program was Dr. J. T. Williams. His wife, Louise, organized the event with the help of the teachers, students, parents and many other sponsors and assistants. Due to their efforts more than $5,000 was raised for the school.

I resigned from St. Patrick School at the end of the school year in order to write my memoirs – this book. I am grateful for the opportunity I had to teach in this wonderful school. I made many friends there and cherish the times we had together.

When I finally resigned from St. Past in 2003, I felt that I had accomplished what I set out to do: establish a fine choral program with the students from grades 7-12. I had a lot of private students, and I was content to teach them, and do what my friend, Dr. David Blake, neurologist, told me: Be sure and play a lot of bridge and work crossword puzzles to keep from having Alzheimer's! I took him seriously and do so still. Perhaps the real reason for resigning was to write my memoirs. I had been urged by many people to do so, and I needed the time to reconstruct events in my mind and put on paper the past 64 years.

CHAPTER 15: A TRIBUTE
"With a Song in Her Heart"

On October 22, 2005, I was completely surprised and completely humbled by an evening titled, "A Tribute to Coralie Runyon Jones." R. Dennison Keller, one of my marvelous students so many years ago at Ripley High School, had worked for more than five years to organize this gala evening of remembrance. Denny has had a fabulous career as director of many state beauty pageants, and has served as a judge in the Miss America Pageant. He, along with his daughter, Caroline Keller Reece, wrote and produced a show entitled, "With a Song in Her Heart." Presented at the Maysville Community College, it had all the excitement of a Broadway show: roving spotlights, a huge screen upon which were projected pictures of my parents, my children when they were small, my sisters, my homes in New Mexico and Arizona, and pictures of me when I was very young.

Many of my former students had come from places near and far to offer their tributes. I was flabbergasted when my sisters, Bonnie Kuhn, from Phoenix, Arizona and Martha Jay, from Pecos, Texas, appeared on stage in a "Sister Act." They had arrived in Maysville several days earlier, staying at a motel and attending rehearsals for this fabulous show. They went to great lengths to keep me from discovering that they were there. My nephew, Jim, from Phoenix and his wife, Judi, had also traveled across the country to be with us that night.

After introductory remarks by Denny and Caroline, the emcees, the Limestone Chorale, directed by John Ziegler, presented "With a Song in My Heart." This was followed by my sisters, Bonnie and Martha, presenting their act of remembrance. After the singing of "All My Trials" by the Chorale, two of my former students from Orangeburg, Richard Zeigler and Winn Turner, gave recollections from 1941. The Chorale then sang a number I had used with the Orangeburg Junior High Chorus at contest, Mozart's "Cradle Song."

The Maysville Years segment followed with Catherine Clarke,

outstanding soprano and performer from New York City, sang "Love is Where You Find it," a number she had used in contests when she was my student, winning first place every time. After that, a picture of John K. Farris, former band director of Maysville High School, appeared on the bug screen as a letter was read that he had sent for the occasion. After a duet, "People Will Say We're in Love" by Betty Fraley Rhodes and Bob Myers, Connie and Randy took to the stage to give "Memories of Mother."

The Ripley Years included the Ripley High School's recording of "The last Words of David" and "I Hear a Song." Two former students at Ripley, Eileen Davis Marshall and Marcele Germann Bowen, replied with "We Hear a Song."

Home Again–Mason County featured several former students from that school: Phillip Stephen Manning spoke of the first choir there, and Christy Clarke recounted the trip to England. Melissa Turner Weaver, who had won first place in Vienna in vocal competition, sang "Laurie's Song" followed by Dr. Richard Blake, who had won first place in the national competition in Washington, D.C., who sang, "This is the Moment." The Chorale then presented "The

Me, Randy, my granddaughters Catherine and Hillary Ford, and Connie on the night of the Tribute.

chapter fifteen

Neighbor's Chorus."

New Endeavors brought Priscilla Browning, my wonderful accompanist with the Mason County Choir, who came from her home in Ithaca, New York, to talk about the Limestone Youth Orchestra's years, and presented me with a jacket with Mason County High School on the back!

The next segment, Once and Again, featured James Ross Beane, my marvelous friend from Morehead State University days, who read a letter from Robert Page who now teaches at Carnegie Mellon that recalled the occasions we three spent together in the choral field. Renee Rosser Koehn, who now lives in Nashville, Tennessee, sang Mozart's "Alleluia" and the Chorale sang "I Will Praise Thee."

One of the most incredible acts was the one that followed featuring my former accompanists. Each sat to play a few bars of "The Can Can" until being pushed off the bench by the next, never faltering in the tune. These amazing accompanists were: James Clarke, Bedouin Ullery, Suzan Ross, Amber Lee Abel, Kristen Carlson, Bettsy Kalb, Priscilla Browning, Kathy Wright Orner, Debbie King DeHoag, and Marcele Germann Bowen.

The spectacular show concluded with "The Best of Times" sung by former students. They included: Michael Bolden, Marla Kalb Sowers, Kent Kalb, Karen Ross Myers, Mary K. Williams Branch, Mickey Wallingford Wilson, Noel Weaver, Maria Harrison Jones, Gary Biddle, Patty Grigson Graves, Zach Ullery, C.J. Hunter, Chiara Fulton Harris, Cathie Phillips Insko, Michael Clarke, Marla Wilson Brock, and the entire company. Members of the Limestone Chorale were: Mary R. Anderson, Gisela Carlson, Maggie Sledd, Kaye Browning, Michael Clarke, Randall Dennison, Patty de Vaughan, Leslie Fox, Marty Frankenhoff, Sue Ellen Grannis, Toni McHugh, Rita McHugh, Cathie Insko, Louise Moneyhon, Roseanne Palmer, Marion Russell, Saundra Stevens, David Sugerbaker, Genrose Turner, Winn Turner, Carrie Jacobs, Andrew Young, Tyler Mains, George Day, Jerry Zeigler, Richard Zeigler, Robert Blake, Bedouin Ullery, Suzan Ross, Caroline Reece and John Denham.

Many people and organizations contributed to the success

of this marvelous evening: Phillip Manning, John Zeigler, Norma Linville, C.J. Hunter IV, Dawn and Christopher Browning, Lou Browning, Robert Roe, Ann Belcher, Joni Powers, the Museum Center, Mark Wallingford, Bill Jones, Mike and Myra Hardy, The Maysville Players, Debbie Lewis, David Clarke, The Ledger-Independent, Jonathan Frazure, Lynn Pfeffer, Barb Campbell, Maysville Community and Technical College, Laura Rains, Jackie Hall, Bob Hendrickson, Mary Ann Kearns, The Downing Performing Arts Academy, the Gordon Lee and Elsie Downing Fund for the Arts, and the Limestone Youth Orchestra.

At the very end of the evening's performance the baton was handed to me and the entire cast joined the audience in singing, "My Old Kentucky Home."

A reception that followed, held at the Maysville Country Club, was icing on the cake. The Mayor of Maysville, David Cartmell, presented me with a proclamation naming October 22, 2005, "Coralie Runyon Jones Day." There were many remarks of congratulation and best wishes made during the evening, and e-mails and messages were read that had been sent from students who were unable to attend the festivities. Steve Moss, serving in the Kentucky National Guard in Kuwait, sent a message of remembrance, as did other students from many places. I shall always treasure the memories of students who have me such great pleasure and their accomplishments. My wish for them is to continue their own search for excellence in all their endeavors.

Coda: Appendices

Developing Superior Choirs

   A great choral program starts in the junior high or middle school. I always insisted on teaching in this area and discovered several ways of building musicianship:

   1. Classify the voices carefully. Always be alert to changes. Listen to each student often. Have the girls sing soprano and alto interchangeably

   2. Understand the boys' voices. The cambiata usually has only four notes. Find music that accommodates this. There is a lot available. Use the "Alleluia" from the Bach cantata, "For Us a child Is Born" and the "Gloria" from the Vivaldi "Gloria." Do not use music that is beyond the reach of beginning baritones.

An early piano lesson for my granddaughter Augusta.

3. Teach correct breathing to all students.

4. Acquire a drumstick for each student. Have the students tap the melody on a book while keeping the basic beat with the foot.

5. Teach the keyboard. Each student is required to make his own keyboard of three octaves according to the dimensions of the actual keys. The black keys are pasted on. Teach the students to play. It can be done!

6. Develop within the students a sense of absolute pitch:

Identify the placement of A = 440 on the bridge of the nose. Have the students touch the bridge of the nose while sounding their "A." The students must enter the classroom in absolute silence, thinking an "A." They sound it only when the teacher directs them to do so when all are assembled in the room. After a while of adhering to this, an absolute "A" will be produced. Intervals are then taught in the same way — touching another place on the head for a third, an octave, a fourth, and a fifth.

7. Always use good literature with these young voices.

8. Invite a guest clinician to do a workshop and concert. Prepare the literature ahead of time. The results are amazing!

High School Choir Techniques

1. Always be teaching voice. Teach the breathing, posture, and formation of vowels necessary for a good tone.

2. Demand absolute attention at all times.

3. Always use literature of the finest quality, the finest composers, the major works that are possible with the teenage voices.

4. Teach phrases instead of measures.

5. Conduct voice classes after school. I always use the Italian songs in order to teach proper vowel formation. This works wonders.

6. Have many ensembles within the choir.

7. Organize madrigal groups, singing in Italian, English, and French.

8. Pay attention to proper diction at all times.

9. Provide opportunities for the students to attend choral

clinics with eminent conductors.

    10. As a teacher always seek to study in the summer from the best in the choral field.

Honors Received

1959 – Appointed to the music selection committee for contests by the Ohio Music Educators Association.

1960 – Commended by the First Christian Church, "in deep appreciation for her contributions to the spiritual enrichment of the congregation through music," 1942-1960/

1969 – Served as musical director of "The Legend of Daniel Boone," outdoor drama performed in Harrodsburg, Kentucky.

1970 – Selected as an Outstanding Educator in America.

1971 – Named "Outstanding Woman of the Year" by the University of Kentucky Association of Women.

1973 – Selected as one of 50 outstanding women of America honored at the Emma Willard School in Troy, New York.

1974 – Recognized as one of the outstanding choral conductors in the United States, ceremony held in Innsbruck, Austria.

1979 – Named "Lady of the Year" by the Beta Sigma Sorority.

1979-80 – Received plaque of commendation for service as president of the Kentucky Choral Directors of America.

1980 – Received citation from the Music Teachers National Association as teacher of Richard Alan Blake, national winner in voice, March 17, 1980, in Washington, D.C.

1981 – Received certificate of appreciation for an in recognition of contributions and loyalty to the Commonwealth of Kentucky from Governor John T. Brown, Jr., November 20, 1981.

1983 – Received "Outstanding Service to Education" award from Maysville Community College.

1992 – Selected Kentucky's "Teacher of the Year."

1997 – Received commendation from the Vestry of the Maysville Church of the Nativity for "enriching the music and worship in the ten years of service, providing strong leadership, extraordinary results and great musical instruction."

1998-99 – Named "Teacher of the Month" at St. Patrick School.

2004 – Coralie Runyon Jones Music Library founded by Richard Zeigler, my former student in 1941-42.

2005 – Named one of the outstanding women in America by Who's Who.

Other:

• Served as chairman of the Kentucky All-State Chorus and also the Kentucky All-State Orchestra.

• Received certificate of appreciation from the Kentucky Department of Education for continued service in the teaching profession.

• The first "Messiah" sing-in was dedicated to me, "whose many years of teaching in both the public and private sector helped mold the musical quality of the area." The sing-in was sponsored by the Maysville-Mason County Arts Commission.